# The End
# of the War

*Hitler's Werewolves*

*Massacre at Malmedy*

# The End of the War

## EUROPE: APRIL 15–MAY 23, 1945

### CHARLES WHITING

STEIN AND DAY/*Publishers*/New York

# ACKNOWLEDGEMENTS

I would like to thank the following for their information, given to me in interviews or by means of correspondence:

*German:* Grand Admiral Dönitz, Admiral Frisius, General Fahrmbacher, Major Teske.

*American:* General Clarke, General Gavin, Ambassador Eisenhower.

*British:* General Sir Kenneth Strong, General Sir Brian Horrocks, Lt. Colonel Hankey, Major Howarth, Sergeant Jones.

First published in 1973
Copyright © 1973 by Charles Whiting
Library of Congress Catalog Card No. 73–79132
All rights reserved
Printed in the United States of America
Stein and Day/*Publishers*/Scarborough House, Briarcliff Manor, N.Y. 10510
ISBN 0–8128–1605–6

# Contents

# Illustrations

# Maps

## Drawn by Patrick Leeson

# Foreword

This is the story of a battle and its aftermath.

It was a great battle—perhaps the last great battle to be fought by the British Army—and it resulted in success for its commander, Field-Marshal Montgomery. A whole German army surrendered and this led to the complete breakdown of the entire enemy defence facing the Western Allies; total surrender followed soon afterwards.

But it was a battle waged under conditions totally unlike those attending any prior to it and for objectives which could not be revealed to the general public till years later, indeed at the time not even to the American and British soldiers who actually fought it.

For it was a battle designed not only to beat the German enemy, but also a new enemy from the East—the erstwhile Russian ally! Its aim was to break through the German defences on the River Elbe so that Montgomery's men could fight their way to the Baltic coast and thus prevent the advancing Russians from moving westwards into North-West Europe.

As if this circumstance did not make the battle unusual enough, it was made even more curious by the grudging approval that Britain's other ally, the United States, gave to its execution. Then the Supreme Commander of the Anglo-American armies in Europe, General Dwight D. Eisenhower, the idol of the British and American peoples, had set his face rigidly against any measure which might be interpreted as provocative or anti-Russian by the Soviet dictator Joseph Stalin whom he fondly called 'UJ'—'Uncle Joe'.

In that spring of 1945 the two authors of the military and political policy which led to the 'Finale in Flensburg', Field-Marshal Montgomery and the British Prime Minister, Win-

1

ston Churchill, were like prophets in the wilderness, misunderstood and often detested by their friends and closest associates. The campaign which they were to engineer was to be a source of irritation and suspicion, not only to the Russians who guessed its real intention, but also to their American 'cousins across the sea' who did understand the need for it.

And in the end it was a failure—a brilliant one—but a failure all the same. For Churchill, who saw the vital political necessity underlying the battle, did not succeed in using it to lay the foundations of a new and better world, free from the fear of war. Nor did the man who fought it gain the kudos he expected from it. He ended it with a great victory, but the gains of that victory were frustrated for him, as for Churchill, by the man they both affected to love and admire so much—Dwight D. Eisenhower.          •

# Introduction

'Clearly Berlin is the main prize.'
*Dwight D. Eisenhower,*
*15 September, 1944*

On that chill March day in Rheims the Supreme Commander had been working on the problem since he had arrived at his office in the former boys' technical school at 7.45 am. He had seen his Chief-of-Staff 'Beetle' Smith briefly and then addressed himself to the cables waiting for him in Smith's blue-leather folder labelled 'For Eisenhower's Eyes Only'. A brief glance at the uppermost two cables of the score or so in the folder convinced him that now at last the time had come to act.

Outside, the ancient French locomotives in the shunting yards at the back of the bullet-pocked *Gare* clattered back and forth. Further up the sloping cobbled back street in which the Supreme Headquarters were located in what the GI clerks called the 'little red schoolhouse', the two-and-a-half-ton supply trucks of the Red Ball Express rumbled through the narrow streets. But Eisenhower did not hear their persistent rumble nor the clatter of the locomotives as he sat in his bare little office on the second floor. His mind was concentrated solely on the two cables and the decision they demanded from him: a decision, which he realized might be the most important he would ever take in Europe.

The one cable was from the man who had 'discovered' him, as some of the more envious of his fellow general officers were wont to describe what had happened to the obscure lieutenant-colonel in 1940, General Marshall, the US Chief-of-Staff in Washington. In it Marshall, who back in 1942 would have dearly loved to have had Eisenhower's job for himself but who had been forced to stay in Washington by Roosevelt, asked what Eisenhower now intended to do. The German front in the West looked as if it might fall apart at any moment. Did

3

he perhaps think of advancing rapidly on, say, the Nuremberg–Linz or Karlsruhe–Munich axes to prevent any organized German resistance being formed in the Bavarian–Austrian Alps?

The other was from Field-Marshal Montgomery. Monty's cable was not a query; it was a demand for approval to drive his British 21st Army Group and the attached US 9th Army up the German autobahn into Berlin.

He could not delay making up his mind any longer. Already his armies had crossed the Rhine from Wesel to Oppenheim and were beginning to break out of their bridgeheads into the flat German plains beyond, pushing back the enemy without difficulty. On this day, 28 March, 1945, he must decide on his strategy for the rest of the Allied campaign in Europe; and more important, what the ultimate objective of his victorious armies would be.

Five years before the obscure infantry lieutenant-colonel, as he was then, had returned from duty in the Philippines to take up a staff appointment, feeling in some way that his career was over; in thirty years in the US Army he had not risen higher than a colonel. Indeed so little was known of him that when he took part in an exercise, a photo caption of him at the time listed him as 'Lieut-Colonel D. D. Ersenbeing'. But in the following months things moved fast. He was promoted to Brigadier-General. Marshall ordered him to Washington on to his staff. And then in 1942 had recommended him as Supreme Commander for Europe over the heads of 366 other generals senior to him. That June he told his wife Mamie over the phone: 'Looks like I'm going to London next week. I'm going to be in command there.' 'In command of what?' Mamie had asked. '*Of the whole shebang!*' he had replied in triumph.

That had been three years ago. Now he had command over the most awesome military machine the world had ever seen. Over the last thirty-six months his career had been like that of a twentieth-century Grant, whose power was multiplied a thousand times by virtue of the fact that he commanded the greatest army that his country had ever sent to war. And during that time he had taken many a hard decision: decisions in North Africa, Sicily, London, Normandy, Versailles, day after day, week after week, year after year, decisions which had hardened and matured him and steeled him against the carping criticism of the envious, the inferior, the impotent.

Yet sitting there alone, smoking another of the sixty cigarettes he chain-smoked each day, he knew that the decision he

4

must make this day could only bring down a violent barrage of criticism from all sides upon him.

He knew what Omar Bradley, the commander of his 12th Army Group expected of him. 'Brad' had told him often enough these last three months since the Ardennes fiasco how *he* thought the campaign should be run once the Rhine, the last great natural barrier into Germany, had been crossed. Brad, who had been a cadet with him at West Point in the famous 'generals' class of '15 and had served him loyally ever since North Africa, wanted the main thrust to be made through central Germany with the last action of the war a deep drive into Bavaria to be undertaken by 'Georgie' Patton's fast-moving 3rd Army.

Eisenhower knew that Bradley considered the central and southern thrusts necessary to prevent any fanatical last-ditch Nazi stand in the Bavarian Alps. Seven days before, Bradley's HQ had made just this point in its study entitled *Re-orientation of Strategy*. But he knew too that Bradley's insistence on the importance of the right wing drive was not motivated solely by military thinking. Brad had suffered a bad blow when his armies had been caught off guard during the German surprise attack in the Ardennes in the previous December. He also felt that his honour and that of the US Army had been sullied by the fact that Montgomery had been given command of the northern half of the battle, controlling more US troops than he did. Soon after the battle had been successfully concluded, Bradley had told him unequivocally: 'You must know, Ike, that I cannot serve under Montgomery ... for if Montgomery goes in over me, I will have lost the confidence of my command.'

Eisenhower thought of the rumpus that the Ardennes had created between Montgomery and Bradley. Things had been so bad that he had been forced to bring the maximum pressure to bear on Montgomery. Through the intermediary of Montgomery's Chief-of-Staff, Freddie de Guingand, he had let him know that it was either 'him or me'; in other words, if Montgomery did not back down in his demands to take over the ground war as senior land commander he, Eisenhower, would ask to be sent back home.

Now a little less than three months later the same old personality problems were cropping up again. He took another look at Montgomery's terse nine paragraph cable which spelled out his desire 'to drive hard for the Elbe' and from there 'by autobahn to Berlin, I hope'.

He dropped it back in the folder. It made him feel 'like a

horse with a burr under his saddle'. As always, Montgomery wanted the kudos of victory for himself alone. Monty knew as well as he did that there were only supplies enough for one major offensive. If he were to be allowed to drive to Berlin, then Bradley's drive in the centre and the south would have to be weakened, perhaps even cancelled altogether. There simply could not be two main pushes eastwards.

Montgomery, he felt—as he was to tell a reporter after the war—'had become so personal in his efforts to make sure that the Americans—and me, in particular—got no credit, that, in fact, we hardly had anything to do with the war, that I finally stopped talking to him'.

As he mulled the problem over he wondered what the verdict of history would be if he gave Montgomery his head; wouldn't the wrong people be gaining the credit for the Allied victories in the field? Hadn't Bradley told him that the 'prestige of the US Army' was involved? What would history's judgement be on himself? And there was his own future to be considered when the war was finished. After all, virtually every successful American general from Washington, through Jackson and Grant, right up to Pershing himself had been offered political office once the battle was over.

Shortly after three that afternoon. Eisenhower approved the draft of the first cable outlining his new strategy. It ran in three phases. The initial: 'immediate operations are designed to encircle and destroy the enemy defending the Ruhr'. The second phase envisaged a link up of Bradley's force on the River Elbe somewhere in central Germany, which would be followed by the third one in which Bradley would then support Montgomery in a drive to the Baltic coast.

One hour later the new plan was encoded and was ready for dispatch to 'UJ'. But it went out under a somewhat more formal title as a 'Personal Message to Marshal Stalin.' Two hours later the other cables were ready for dispatch to the two men who had cabled him the day previously, Marshall and Montgomery.

In the cable to his boss, he wrote that he had communicated with Stalin 'on the question of where we should aim to link up' and suggested the Leipzig–Dresden axis as the direction of the major thrust eastwards because it offered the 'shortest route to present Russian positions' and would also overrun 'the one remaining industrial area in Germany to which ... the High Command Headquarters and Ministries are reported moving'.

The cable went out at 7 pm. Five minutes later the third

cable followed it, addressed to Field-Marshal Montgomery. 'As soon as you have joined hands with Bradley (beyond the Ruhr) ... the Ninth US Army will revert to Bradley's command ... Bradley will be responsible for mopping up ... the Ruhr and with the minimum delay will deliver his main thrust on the axis Erfurt–Leipzig–Dresden to join hands with the Russians.' Perhaps when Montgomery reached the Elbe it might be 'desirable for the Ninth Army to revert to your operational control again to facilitate the crossing of that obstacle'.

A little while later Eisenhower collected his coat and went down the private staircase to the one-time school reception hall. At the door the two MPs, one British, one American, saluted smartly. His car was waiting to take him to the handsome château in the centre of Rheims which had once been owned by one of the local champagne barons but which Eisenhower now called his temporary home.

In five minutes he would be with his 'unofficial official family', as it was called—Butch, his Navy PR man, Tex, the booming-voiced captain who kept his records in order, Telek, his dog, Mickey, his former bell-hop sergeant, who was his orderly, Kay, the only Britisher among them, who had recently become a lieutenant in the US Army.

The decision had been made. Henceforth Mongomery's role would be limited merely 'to protect Bradley's northern flank'; and the last optimistic words which Eisenhower had added to the final draft of the cable to him would be of little consolation to the Englishman who at this moment still felt he was Berlin-bound with the main Allied thrust: 'As you say the situation looks good.'

It didn't! The role of the British Army had been reduced to that of a flank guard in the last decisive battle; and more important, in all three cables sent out that day, there had been no mention of Berlin.

# I

# DECISION ON THE ELBE

'There is only one thing worse than fighting with allies—
and that is fighting without them!'

*Winston Churchill,*
*March, 1945*

# I

# No Road to Berlin

## 11–15 APRIL, 1945

'That place (Berlin) has become, as far as I am concerned, nothing but a geographical location.'

*Eisenhower to Montgomery,*
*30 March, 1945*

1

They reached the river in the early evening. On the high ground east of the little town of Schönebeck the Shermans came to a halt. Gratefully the drivers switched off their engines. On the decks the infantry and the tank commanders in their leather helmets clambered stiffly to the ground. Behind them the odd house was still burning in Schönebeck and from somewhere in the distance came the persistent crack of a rifle followed by the high-pitched burr of a grease-gun. But the men had no eyes or ears for what was going on behind them. Their attention was on the river which had been their objective for these last two hectic weeks of fighting and travelling. They had made it!

While the men relaxed, their commander, Major James Hollingsworth, strode a little further up the hill, unfastening his binoculars as he went. The Major looked like something out of a Hollywood movie with his twin Colts strapped low on his hips and a Thompson sub-machine-gun slung over his shoulder. But Hollingsworth's appearance was not just show. It was said that he had killed a hundred and fifty enemy soldiers and only three hours before he had shot and killed two SS men who had had the audacity to attempt to hold up his advance.

He raised the glasses and focused them on the river. Gleaming in the evening light, it stretched placidly from one bank to the other at a distance of perhaps 500 feet. A tough obstacle when those apparently innocent bushes growing low down on the bank at the far side might be hiding enemy soldiers ready to defend this last natural barrier to the bitter end.

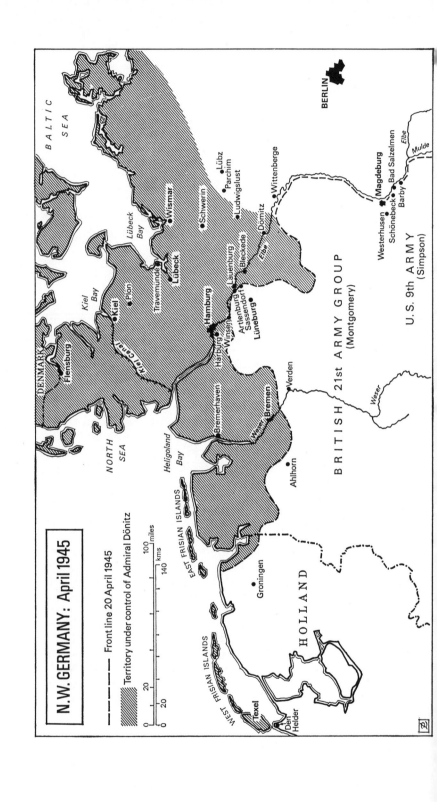

# N.W. GERMANY: April 1945

------- Front line 20 April 1945

Territory under control of Admiral Dönitz

BALTIC SEA

DENMARK

Flensburg

Kiel Bay

Kiel Canal

Kiel

Plön

Lübeck Bay

Travemünde

Lübeck

Wismar

Schwerin

Lübz

Parchim

Ludwigslust

Wittenberge

Dömitz

Elbe

Lauenburg

Bleckede

Artlenburg

Sassendorf

Lüneburg

Hamburg

Harburg

Winsen

Verden

Bremerhaven

Bremen

Weser

Ahlhorn

NORTH SEA

Heligoland Bay

EAST FRISIAN ISLANDS

WEST FRISIAN ISLANDS

Texel

Den Helder

Groningen

HOLLAND

BERLIN

Magdeburg

Westerhusen

Schönebeck

Bad Salzelmen

Barby

Mulde

Elbe

U.S. 9th ARMY
(Simpson)

BRITISH 21st ARMY GROUP
(Montgomery)

0     20     40     60     80     100 miles

0   20   40   60   80  100  120  140 kms

Abruptly his heart missed a beat. A steel and concrete structure had inserted itself into the bright circle of glass. *A bridge!* There was actually a bridge still standing over the river! He stared at it hard. It was too good to be true. Containing his joy, he studied its outline and then switched his gaze to the road that ran over it. It was packed with fleeing enemy vehicles: nose to tail, cumbersome wood-burning trucks, their decks camouflaged with branches; heavy self-propelled guns, their long hooded guns hanging down in front as if they were too heavy for the iron monsters; pathetic little horse-drawn carts, packed high with furniture and mattresses, as protection against air attack, and a score of other personal possessions that civilians always take with them when they flee; and everywhere men and women, some in civilian clothes, others in uniform, plodding steadily eastwards to safety. There was no time to lose. With luck and a hell of a lot of speed on his part, he might just capture the first bridge across the Elbe.

On that Wednesday evening, two weeks after General Eisenhower had made up his mind in Rheims, Colonel Disney, CO of the 67th Armoured Infantry, received the news of 'Hollingsworth's Bridge' almost at once. And for Hollingsworth's CO it was a moment of great personal triumph.

Two days before he had been summoned to divisional HQ and ushered immediately into the presence of the 2nd Armoured Division's Commander, Major-General Isaac White. White, head of the Army's biggest armoured division, which formed a column more than 72 miles long when it moved into action, did not waste words, Hardly had Disney saluted when the General said, 'Right, take off east!'

Colonel Disney, who had been long enough with the 2nd, nicknamed 'Hell on Wheels', to know White's laconic orders was this time too punch-drunk from the previous eleven days' fighting and driving to think straight. He looked blankly at the other man and stammered, 'But what's the objective, sir?'

White's answer was limited to one word: *'Berlin!'* Now on this Wednesday afternoon after an unparalleled fighting road march of 73 miles, a record that not even Patton's much-vaunted 4th Armoured Division, could beat, Disney's regiment had reached its objective in just over twenty-four hours. And now as the light began to fade, it looked to a jubilant Disney as if Hollingsworth might do what Hoge had done the month before on the Rhine at Remagen—take a German bridge on the run before the enemy were aware what was happening to them.

Ordering Hollingsworth to hurry on, he flashed General White a message which was as laconic as the one the Com-

13

mander had given him two days before. It read, 'We are on the Elbe.'

Standing there on the heights above the river, Hollingsworth realized that everything now depended upon the speed at which he could get his men down to the bridge, Swiftly he outlined his makeshift plan to his two company commanders, Captains James Starr and Jack Knight.

It was all haste and improvisation. Hollingsworth did not know that the Elbe had not been taken by storm in nearly a century and a half. But even if he had, he would not have cared; that evening history was here and now.

'They're moving along the road running north to south into Bad Salzelmen,' he told the two officers. 'Then they swing east at the road junction, head into Schönebeck and cross the bridge. Our only hope is to charge into Bad Salzelmen and grab the junction. Now here's what we'll do. When we get to the junction, your company, Starr, will peel off and block the road, holding the Germans coming up from the south. I'll join on to the rear of the German column that has already swung east into Schönebeck, and follow it across the bridge. Knight, you come up behind. We've got to get that bridge. *And by God, we're going to do it!*'

'Turn 'em over!' Hollingsworth roared into his tank mike. The drivers gunned their exhausts. Blue flames shot out of the tank exhausts. There was a creak and rattle of tracks. The first tank lurched forward. They were on their way.

Hatches battened down, the American tanks hit Bad Salzelmen before the startled German infantry were aware that they had been attacked. At the same moment Starr's men opened up as a feint. Abruptly everything was transformed into chaos and confusion. On the bridge the fleeing German vehicles started to speed up. But contrary to the Germans' expectations they were following up right behind the end of the German column in a daring attempt to fool the enemy. As Hollingsworth's tank turned a corner, a German Mark V was waiting for him. Its gun swung hurriedly round to bear upon the Sherman. But Hollingsworth's gunner, Staff Sergeant Cooley, with his electrically operated turret, was quicker. The Sherman jerked violently. A long red and yellow flame shot out of the 75-mm. The panzer slewed into a wall, as if lifted by some gigantic invisible hand. A burst of flame shot from within it. Hollingsworth pushed on. But the going was getting tougher. Everywhere damaged and burning vehicles blocked the way in the narrow cobbled street. And everywhere there was the sharp crack and shower of redhot flames which heralded the

14

*Panzerfaust,* the one-shot German bazooka, which could be used to great advantage against tanks in the narrow street.

Hollingsworth's luck held. Now he was a matter of a couple of hundred yards away from the bridge and his tank was still undamaged. Ahead he spotted the maze of 6-foot-high concrete walls which had been built around the bridge's entrance to slow down any vehicle approaching it from the west. It was a primitive but effective defence. The approach to the entrance was going to be like running an obstacle race.

Hollingsworth sprang from the turret and, holding his tank telephone in one hand (attached to the back of the tank) and a ·45 pistol in the other, began to talk the driver through the barriers, directing Sergeant Cooley's fire at the same time.

Suddenly a thin stream of red and yellow flame split the darkness. There was the vicious noise of metal striking stone. A solid shot 57-mm anti-tank shell struck the road a few yards away from him. A dozen razor-sharp slivers of stone struck him in the face. Hollingsworth reeled back, bleeding heavily and blinded by blood.

With an impatient jerk of the back of his free hand he wiped the blood from his eyes and continued to work the Sherman through the barriers, moving ever closer to the bridge. The Sherman bumped into a jeep, which suddenly loomed up out of the gloom. Now the road to the bridge was really blocked. Cursing angrily, he abandoned the tank and called up a handful of infantry. Doggedly he led them ever closer to the bridge, fighting from barrier to barrier.

Seventy yards—60 yards. The Germans were fighting back desperately now. They knew the vital importance of the bridge too. The night air was thick with lead. Fifty yards. Hollingsworth was hit in the left knee. He staggered. Blinded by his own blood, his head hanging groggily, waves of pain shooting up from his knee, he moved on another pace. And another. Then he gave in. He could take no more; and the German fire was becoming more intense by the second. 'Pull back,' he called weakly, taking a last look at the bridge which they had come so far to capture. It was 40 yards away. Once over it and the 2nd Armoured Division might have been in Berlin in eleven hours.

At dawn on 12 April, 1945 the Germans blew up the Schöne-beck bridge.

## II

On that bright April morning Patton's HQ woke early. When he had first taken over the 3rd Army in the spring of 1944, General Patton had insisted on early breakfasts for staff officers and that his people take care of their personal ablutions before eight o'clock. But that had been in the beginning. Over the last eight months of combat in Europe from which he had emerged as General 'Blood and Guts' Patton, America's most successful fighting general, he had relaxed his grip a little. The 'team'—General Gay, Colonels Harkins, Codman and the rest—had been allowed to enjoy a more civilized, leisurely existence, with mess waiters in white coats, valuable table silver and damask tablecloths, with choice wines and good steaks whenever Codman, a born provider, could get his hands on them.

But on that particular spring morning in the gloomy German town of Bad Hersfeld, not too far from Frankfurt where the 3rd Army HQ was located in the middle of a former German Army training centre, the brass rose and breakfasted early and got about their daily business with alacrity; today the big brass was coming. Both Eisenhower, the Supreme Commander and Bradley, Commander of the 12th Army Group to which the 3rd Army belonged, were coming to visit; and in the case of the Supreme Commander this was his first visit to his most aggressive, and most troublesome, subordinate in nearly a month.

Patton was well prepared for them. Eisenhower's special trailer—that status symbol of high rank in World War II—was ready and waiting for him. Codman, one-time buyer for a major American wine firm, had ensured that there would be a fine dinner 'laid on' for that evening; and he, Patton, had personally taken care of the day's itinerary so that Ike would see all that was worth seeing in the Third Army area.

Yet in spite of everything Patton was worried. Two weeks before he had ordered a small raiding force from his favourite 4th Armoured Division to break through the German lines near Aschaffenburg and fight its way to an American POW camp at Hammelburg. Under the command of a twenty-four-year-old captain named Baum, assisted by Patton's favourite aide, Major Al Stiller, who had been his tank sergeant in World War I, the 300-man force had actually fought its way through 60 miles of enemy-held territory and liberated the

1,000-odd US prisoners held in the camp.

After that nothing more had been heard of the force and Patton had regretfully been forced to conclude that Task Force Baum had been wiped out. Now he feared that Ike might give him a hard time on account of the raid. Not because it had failed; that could happen in wartime. It was the luck of the great game—as Patton saw war. No, because he had ordered the raid in the first place.

Ostensibly he had ordered the raid to fool the Germans as to the direction of the 3rd Army's advance once it had crossed the River Main, but Patton knew Ike wouldn't believe that. He would know the real reason for the raid—that Patton had wanted to liberate his favourite son-in-law, Colonel John Waters, who had been captured in North Africa two years earlier and was believed to be imprisoned in the Hammelburg Camp.[1]

That was why he had risked Stiller's life in the dangerous enterprise. Naturally Ike wouldn't have said anything if the raid had succeeded. But it had failed and, to compound the felony, Patton had sacked a SHAEF[2] press censor who had passed the news of the raid to the press, although he had absolutely no authority over the SHAEF people. Ike wouldn't like the sacking, especially as 'Butch', Captain Butcher, his PR man, was always jealous in his defence of the press people and 'Butch', Patton thought bitterly, had Ike's ear like all those canteen commandos at SHAEF. Ike would surely know about the sacking.

The morning passed easily enough. Patton took Bradley and Eisenhower to visit an industrial salt mine at the little town of Merkers upon which two days before two soldiers of the 385th Infantry had stumbled and found to their amazement that it was full of gold to the value of $250,000,000 and looted art works from all over Europe to which no one had dared so far to attach a price tag.

A German civilian had taken them down the 2,000-foot shaft leading to the mine, and as the rickety old lift had descended into the gloom at an alarming rate, Patton had not been able to repress his sense of humour. Amused at the looks of alarm on his companions' faces as they looked up at the thin wire which supported them, he said poker-faced: 'If that clothes-line should break, promotion in the United States Army would be considerably stimulated.'

1. For full details of the raid, see my *48 Hours To Hammelburg* (Ballantine N.Y.).
2. Supreme Headquarters, Allied Expeditionary Force.

Down below after visiting the various shafts containing treasure trove ranging from Sèvres vases to gold bridgeworks taken from concentration camp victims, the German pointed to a dozen bales of *Reichsmarks* and said they were the Third Reich's last papermoney reserves, adding: 'They will be badly needed to meet the Army payroll.'

Bradley chuckled in the gloom. 'Tell him,' he said to their interpreter, 'that I doubt the German Army will be meeting payrolls much longer.' Then he turned to Patton. 'If these were the old freebooting days, when a soldier kept his loot, Georgie, you'd be the richest man in the world.'

Thereafter they returned to Patton's XII Corps HQ for lunch. Here Eisenhower finally brought up the subject of the firing of the SHAEF censor. But Patton was unperturbed; he felt he could cope with Eisenhower now. 'I knew I was right on that,' he said expansively.

'Well, I'll be damned!' Eisenhower exclaimed. 'Until you said that, maybe you were. But if you're that positive, then I'm sure you're wrong.'

Patton, undismayed, winked across the table at Bradley, his one-time subordinate in North Africa.

The latter laughed and quickly changed the subject. 'But why keep it secret George—what would you do with all that money?'

Patton's face cracked into a thin-lipped smile. Half the 3rd Army, he explained, wanted the money—or the gold part of it—made into medallions. 'One for every sonuvabitch in the Third Army!' The other half wanted it hidden so that when Congress cracked down on army spending after the war, they could drag it out again and buy new weapons.

Eisenhower shook his head in resignation. Turning to Bradley, he said: 'He's always got an answer!'

And thus they chatted, the three most powerful generals in the US Army in Europe, unaware that at that very moment some 4,000 miles away an event was taking place which would make one of them, not only the United States' most powerful field commander but also the most powerful man in Western Europe, whose actions in the next few weeks—completely unrestrained by politicians now—would change the whole face of that Continent. The once so obscure 'Lieutenant-Colonel D. D. Ersenbeing' was at that moment making his first great step on the road to the total control of Allied policy in Europe.

On that particular Thursday morning the President of the United States, Franklin Delano Roosevelt, had no work of any great import to complete. So he relaxed in bed at his summer residence in Warm Springs, Georgia, reading the *Atlanta Constitution* and dabbling a little in a mystery called *The Punch and Judy Murders*. But he could not get interested in a chapter entitled 'Six Feet of Ground'. As he told his coloured maid when she came in: 'I don't feel any too good this morning.' In fact he had not been feeling 'any too good' ever since he had returned from his fateful meeting with Stalin and Churchill at Yalta two months before.

A little later he went downstairs and chatted a while with his female cousins while the lady portraitist Madame Elizabeth Shoumanoff set up her easel ready to carry on a painting she was doing for him which he was going to present to the daughter of his ex-mistress. Finally she draped a navy blue cape around the President's shoulders and began to work.

Time passed. At one o'clock, Roosevelt looked at his watch and commented: 'We've got just fifteen minutes more.'

She nodded and continued working.

Then suddenly her subject touched his temple and let his hand fall abruptly down one side of the big leather armchair.

'Did you drop something?' one of the female cousins asked.

Roosevelt opened his eyes and said softly, 'I have a terrific headache.' Then he slumped over and lost consciousness. The fifteen minutes were up.

Two hours later, propped up in his big bed in the six-room clapboard cottage called the 'Little White House' where he had always been so happy, the man who had controlled the destinies of the United States for so long was dead. When finally at 3.35 pm that afternoon Dr James Paullin of Atlanta closed the dead man's eyes, the open copy of the *Constitution* lay on the table near the bedside. On the front page the headline read, '9th 57 miles from Berlin'.

Roosevelt, during the course of the war, had left the running of the battlefields to the 'military technicians', as he called them a little contemptuously. In Washington there had been a tacit division of labour between himself and the Chief-of-Staff, General Marshall. He took care of the politics, Marshall of the fighting. With his death the equilibrium was upset.

Truman, the Vice-President, who automatically became the new President, had been deliberately kept in the dark by Roosevelt. As a result the only man in the know after 12 April was General Marshall, which meant that henceforth the entire American conduct of the war was shifted to the military sphere, although it was become increasingly clear to such politicians as Churchill and soldiers like Montgomery that the military sphere was becoming less important with each new day; the post-war political situation was now paramount.

But the servicemen were now in charge. General Marshall and Admiral Leahy, Chief-of-Staff to the President and an old comrade of Roosevelt's in World War I, were in such complete control that even if Cordell Hull, of the US State Department, had wished to direct the remaining course of the war along political lines, no one would have listened to him.[3]

Marshall, now the key man in Washington, was concerned almost exclusively with military issues—the problems of how to end the war in Europe efficiently and cheaply with the least loss of life and how to get Soviet Russia in on America's side in the last decisive battle against Japan. All he wanted from Eisenhower now was that he ended the war against the Nazis; the manner of his doing this was Eisenhower's concern. It had always been American military dogma to tell a subordinate what you wanted done and then let him do it in any way he chose as long as it led to success.

From now onwards his one-time protégé in Europe had a completely free hand.

IV

On the same afternoon that Roosevelt died and General Patton was being sick after taking Eisenhower to view the notorious Nazi concentration camp at Ohrdruf Nord, the commander of the US 9th Army, General Simpson, was worried about the position of his front on the River Elbe. 'Big Simp', as his men called him affectionately behind his back,

3. After the war he wrote: 'After Pearl Harbor I did not sit in on meetings concerned with military matters. This was because the President did not invite me to such meetings. I raised the question with him several times ... The question of where the armies would land and what routes they would take across the Continent in the grand military movement to conquer Hitler was a subject never discussed with me.'

knew that the German opposition facing him on the other side of the river was negligible. His 19th Corps, under General McLain, which was lined up on the western bank of the river was 120,000 strong, bigger than the whole US Union Army at Gettysburg, and he figured that the Germans couldn't field anything like that number to oppose him.

As he saw it, there was a thin hard crust of enemy defence on the other side of the water and once that was broken there was nothing to stop him driving for what Ike often called the 'glittering prize of Berlin'.

General Simpson's 9th Army had had a hard campaign. Although it had been the last US Army to be activated in Europe (with the exception of the 15th Army intended for occupation duties), the 9th had endured some very tough fighting during the winter. Unfortunately, for most of the time it had been under the command of Field-Marshal Montgomery, and as a result Simpson felt that his men had received little publicity in either the American or British press.

'Big Simp' felt this was grossly unfair. The papers were always full of Monty's or Blood an' Guts' exploits; never of his. Now, at last, he felt a glorious opportunity to make the headlines. Berlin, the end of the road, was within grabbing distance. And his men were keyed up, ready to fight those last miles with all they'd got in spite of the last two weeks' hard fighting and travelling since they had crossed the Rhine two weeks before. All he needed was a bridge—one single bridge and then, as he had told his staff a few days before: 'Damn, I want to get to Berlin and all you people, right down to the last private, I think, want it too.'

Down on the Elbe, Brigadier-General Sidney Hinds, Commander of the 2nd Division's Combat Command B to which Colonel Disney's regiment belonged, was also worried by the absence of a bridge or bridgehead across the river that afternoon. He knew all about his Army Commander's concern but he was more concerned about the reaction of Isaac White if he didn't get across soon. The Divisional Commander had a nasty tongue when his subordinates failed him; and White confidently expected to be in Berlin within forty-eight hours of crossing the Elbe. In fact, Sid Hinds knew that there was a contingency plan worked out already at 2nd Division HQ, with a map broken up into the six phases of the move from the Elbe all leading to a huge blue swastika superimposed on Berlin and the simple code word 'GOAL'.

The Brigadier-General busied himself with working out a

new attempt at crossing after the failure of Hollingsworth's daring try at Schönebeck. As he saw it, he would use a couple of battalions to bridge the river just south of Magdeburg at the little town of Westerhusen. Once they had formed a bridgehead on the eastern bank, he would throw a pontoon bridge across in short order over which the rest of the 2nd Division would pass. It was a risky business, he knew. The enemy artillery might destroy the bridge or even prevent it being built and then his two battalions of infantry would be at the mercy of the German 12th Army on the other side. But it was a risk he had to take. Every hour he delayed lessened the chances of the 'Hell on Wheels' division beating the Russians to Berlin.

Thus it was that as the light began to fade on 12 April two battalions of infantry started to make their way quietly over the river in small assault boats. Hinds watched them as they moved across the slow-flowing river, stomach tensed for the howl of a mortar, or the crack of an 88-mm cannon. But nothing happened. The first men started to clamber clumsily out of their boats and make their way up the muddy bank on the other side. The crossing was unopposed. Not a shot had been fired.

Hinds grabbed his radio telephone and gave White the good news at once.

White listened and then hung up, only to seize his own direct line to Simpson. Jubilantly he cried, 'We're across!'


v


As the first DUKWs were beginning to transport Hinds' infantry across the Elbe, Patton handed Ike a drink. The Supreme Commander was still shaken by the events of the afternoon and his face was pale and shocked.

'I can't understand the mentality,' he said over the after-dinner drink, 'that would compel these German people to do a thing like that. Our soldiers could never mutilate bodies the way the Germans have.'

'Not all the Germans can stomach it,' Colonel Harkins, Patton's Deputy Chief-of-Staff remarked. 'In one camp we paraded the townspeople through to let them have a look. The mayor and his wife went home and slashed their wrists.'

Time passed and Eisenhower found himself alone with Patton. Suddenly he revealed something which he had not revealed to any other of his subordinate army commanders.

'From a tactical point of view it is highly inadvisable for the American Army to take Berlin and I hope political influence won't cause me to take the city. It has no tactical or strategic value and would place upon the American forces the burden of caring for thousands and thousands of Germans, displaced persons and Allied prisoners of war.'

Patton looked at Eisenhower aghast. 'Ike,' he said, 'I don't see how you figure that out. We had better take Berlin and quick—and on to the Oder.'

The more Patton considered Eisenhower's decision the more concerned he became. Throughout the war he had believed that Berlin was the final target for the campaign in Europe. Now Eisenhower was prepared to abandon it to the Russians, a nation which the aristocratic, independently wealthy Patton, with his string of polo ponies and garage full of expensive automobiles, abhorred. A little later, in the presence of his Chief-of-Staff, General Gay, he tackled Eisenhower once more on the subject. Berlin, he urged, could be taken in forty-eight hours. Eisenhower remained adamant. 'Well, who would want it?' he asked. Patton looked at the younger man. He had known him a long time now. He leaned forward, placed both his hands on Eisenhower's shoulders, and said slowly and carefully: 'I think history will answer that question for you.'


VI


In London Winston Churchill felt as if he'd been 'struck a physical blow' when he heard the news of President Roosevelt's death and was 'overpowered by a sense of deep and irreparable loss'.

His first move was to telephone Bernard Baruch, the American financier who was friend and adviser to both Roosevelt and himself. Baruch happened to be in London, carrying out a mission on which Roosevelt had sent him. 'Do you think I ought to go to Washington?' Churchill asked him.

'No, Winston. I think you ought to stay here on the job.'

He was flying back to Washington immediately himself but he would come and see the Prime Minister before he left. A little later he arrived at 10 Downing Street to find the Prime Minister propped up in bed. Winston was still greatly upset, or so it appeared to Baruch. 'Do you think I ought to go?' he asked again.

Again Baruch reassured him that it would be better that he stayed in London and kept his guiding hand on the war in Europe. Churchill let himself be persuaded, grateful at the back of his mind that he would not have to waste precious time at this vital stage in the war by going to Washington for the funeral. Besides his agile mind was already beginning to envisage how he might turn this sudden tragedy to some advantage for his country.

Churchill's private opinions of Roosevelt have never been recorded. Publicly they seemed to be the greatest of friends and throughout the war at their much publicized meetings they were photographed time and time again in lively discussion—on the deck of the great British battleship, which one day would be the victim of Japanese bombs, on the terrace in North Africa, sitting in the wickerwork chairs at the conference table in the over-furnished conference room at Yalta.

Yet Churchill knew that although Roosevelt was a shrewd domestic politician, he was naïve, gullible and out of his depth when it came to international politics. In particular, as Churchill saw it, Roosevelt, because of his own 'pink' past during the 'New Deal' period, willingly misjudged the Russians. He felt he had gained the friendship of 'Uncle Joe', often at the expense of their 'imperialist friend', Churchill.

But Churchill did not trust Stalin's amiable pipe-smoking image and he felt the Russian dictator had fooled Roosevelt completely. He did not believe that one could work out a *modus vivendi* with Stalin on the basis of compromise, as Roosevelt did; all Stalin understood was power and force. And he, Churchill, had no illusions about Soviet politics. Recent events in Jugoslavia, Greece and Poland had convinced him that Eastern Europe would become one great Russian sphere of influence after the war.

But Roosevelt's attitude to the Russians was not the only thing which gave Churchill cause for disquiet. The scion of a long-established, extremely wealthy American family, Roosevelt looked with suspicion at the old 'Colonial' powers, in particular, Britain; and he had strong views about the future of the British Empire after the war. During the Atlantic Charter Conference he had told Churchill: 'I can't believe that we can fight a war against fascist slavery and at the same time not work to free people all over the world from a backward colonial policy. *The peace cannot include any colonial despotism!*'

Churchill understood immediately what the American

meant. In private he told him, 'Mr President, I believe you are trying to do away with the British Empire.' And in public, he told the audience at the Mansion House dinner in London in 1942: 'We mean to hold our own. I have not become the King's First Minister in order to preside over the liquidation of the British Empire.'

For those in the know, the remark was not aimed at the enemy, but at his erstwhile friend and ally, President Roosevelt.

Now that he was dead, Churchill felt that there might still be some chance to persuade his successor to change the fateful Eisenhower decision of 28 March, which had caused him so much anguish over the Easter weekend. To him it was now clear that Soviet Russia 'had become a mortal danger to the free world ... that a new front must be immediately created against her onward sweep ... that this front in Europe should be as far east as possible (and) that Berlin was the prime and true objective of the Anglo-American armies.'

But in the end he had controlled his anger at what he thought was Eisenhower's colossal blunder. While Brooke, his Chief-of-Staff, who had been Montgomery's Corps Commander in 1940 and was now the latter's chief confidant in London, remarked that the whole Berlin decision was 'due to national aspirations and to ensure that the US effort will not be lost under British command', Churchill capitulated with, 'There is only one thing worse than fighting with allies, *that is fighting without them* !'

The sudden death of the President meant that he might still be able to change the Elbe decision. If he could convince Roosevelt's successor that it was vital to capture Berlin, the Western Allies would have a prestige object in their hands which they could use to bargain with the Russians over the post-war conference tables, even though the German capital would probably lie in the Soviet Zone of Occupation.

Soon Central Europe's major bulwark against communism —Nazi Germany—would be destroyed. Thus when the Americans left, as they surely would, to fight the war in the Pacific, he would be left with a destroyed Germany, a gravely weakened and demoralized France and his own exhausted country to prevent the spread of victorious communism westwards. And time was running out—*fast*! He alone had to try desperately to create a geo-political balance on the ruined continent to oppose post-war Soviet aspirations about which he had no such rosy illusions as had had Roosevelt and his Supreme

Commander Eisenhower.

Truman, the new President, about whom he knew so little and on whom his researchers were hurriedly preparing a dossier, might be his last hope of getting Eisenhower to change his Elbe decision. Thus he began to plan a cable to the man who represented his last hope. This time he would use another approach than he had employed on Easter Sunday when he had first received the news that Eisenhower was to stop on the Elbe. This time he would emphasize to the ex-haberdasher who according to the researchers, was devoted to his daughter Margaret and to playing the piano, that there was going to be a grave problem feeding the Germans once they were beaten.

As he saw it, the Russians would treat their zone of occupation as a close preserve, and as their zone included one of the most important German food producing areas, the Western Allies might be faced with a serious food shortage if the Russians did not co-operate. He would suggest, therefore, that Eisenhower should be directed to send his armies across the Elbe as deeply as possible into Eastern Germany, and that they should not withdraw after the fighting was over unless Stalin agreed to the pooling of all food resources.

In fact, the feeding of the Germans was the least of Churchill's concerns on that Friday, 13 April. But he thought that the further east he was the better he would be able to fight Uncle Joe. Once he was over the River Elbe, the Russians would not get him back again so easily.

VII

The Germans learned of Brigadier-General Sidney Hinds' crossing of the Elbe almost as soon as General Simpson did. On the eastern side of the river forty-five-year-old General Wenck, once Guderian's Chief-of-Staff and the youngest army commander in the *Wehrmacht,* did not hesitate. Although he knew that the war was long lost, the young cadets and officers who had been grouped into élite, if ill-armed, divisions in his 12th Army were eager for their appointment with destiny and death. They piled into their cumbersome wood-burning trucks and tanks and prepared to give battle.

Their attack came in suddenly. Up on the Elbe Colonel Disney, CO of the 67th Armoured Regiment, was watching the bridging operations impatiently, as the engineers inched their way across the 500 feet of placid water under artificial moonlight.[4] Would they never get across? he asked himself time and again. Surely the Krauts would soon realize what they were up to. His foreboding was correct. Abruptly the night air was ripped apart by the crack of an 88-mm shell. A spurt of water shot up in front of him, and another, and another, getting ever closer to the pontoon bridge.

Disney searched the opposite bank for the enemy forward artillery observer. He reasoned that the shells, coming singly rather than in salvoes, were being directed by human rather than mechanical means. But he could see no one.

Persistently, hour after hour, the shells rained down on the crossing site, turning it into a nightmare for the sweating engineers still trying to carry out their task in spite of the steadily mounting casualties. But they were fighting a losing battle. One by one the pontoons were destroyed and as the first light of dawn washed the sky, Disney and his boss knew it would not be long now before they would have to abandon the site. Two hours later General Hinds gave in. With the bridge only 75 yards from the opposite bank, but under tremendous artillery fire, he ordered it abandoned. The 2nd Division's second attempt to establish a firm bridgehead over the Elbe had failed.

But while the 2nd had failed, its running mate, the 83rd Infantry Division under the command of General Macon, had not. The infantry division, which had raced the 'Hell on Wheels' for the honour of crossing the Elbe ever since the operation had started two weeks before, had had tremendous luck. They had driven into the riverside town of Barby, 15 miles south of Magdeburg to find that although the local bridge had already been destroyed, the further bank of the Elbe was *not* defended.

Colonel Edwin 'Buckshot' Crabill of the lead infantry regiment, did not wait for orders. The chance was too good to lose. At once he started getting his men across in the little olive-drab assault boats, persuading the more reluctant with the toe of his boot.

By the afternoon of the 13th, the 83rd was crossing at Barby in large numbers, urged on by Crabill's instructions not to wait to organize, but to get on fanning out on the other side. As DUKWs took fresh infantry across, he bellowed at them, 'Don't wait for someone to tell you what to do! Get over there in any shape you can! If you move *now* you can make it

4. A British device of bouncing the beams of searchlights off low cloud to give light at night.

27

without a shot being fired!' Thus they moved over, hour after hour, without encountering any opposition to speak of.

By that evening three battalions of the 83rd were across and the engineers had finished putting up the first makeshift pontoon bridge, on which they nailed a sign that paid tribute to the new President, who at his first cabinet meeting a short time before had stated that his future plan was 'to continue both the foreign and the domestic policies of the Roosevelt administration'.

It read, 'Truman Bridge, Gateway to Berlin.'

VIII

General Simpson's jubilant voice, excitedly relating the news of the 83rd's crossing, still rang in General Bradley's ears as he replaced the telephone carefully on its cradle. For a while he sat at his desk. The firm bridgehead across the Elbe certainly changed things, he realized. It demanded a decision.

Bradley had come a long way in the last twelve months. A year before he would hardly have dared even dream that he would be commanding forty divisions and advising Ike on what to do next, nor be receiving telephone calls as he had done just the day before, from Winston Churchill, begging him (over Ike's head) not to retreat from the Elbe, as he, Churchill, wished to retain this area to bargain with the Russians. This April, he knew, in spite of his inherent modesty and the common touch which had earned him the name of the 'GIs' General' that he was one of the most important men in Europe.

Yet Simpson's message threatened his new-found status. If Berlin were once more to become the Allies' chief objective, inevitably the advance would be under Montgomery's command and Montgomery, since the Ardennes offensive, had become his bitterest enemy, Eisenhower would place Simpson's 9th Army under the Britisher's command and stop Patton's attack southwards. And what would be the result? Monty would have the kudos of the final victory, and all his work during these last months, his careful working on Eisenhower to accept the central drive rather than Berlin, would be for nothing.

He picked up the phone to Eisenhower. Swiftly he told him Simpson's news about the firm bridgehead at Barby. Eisenhower, in Rheims, listened attentively, then he asked, 'Brad, what do you think it might cost us to break through from the Elbe and take Berlin?'

Bradley considered for a moment. 'I estimate,' he said slowly, 'that it might cost us 100,000 men.'

At the other end of the line Eisenhower was silent. Bradley knew that a glance at the casualty chart which hung prominently in the L-shaped map room at Supreme HQ would show Ike that the Allies were taking extremely light casualties in their drive eastwards; in fact they were the lightest the Anglo-American army had suffered since the campaign had started nearly a year before.[5]

Hurriedly he added, 'It would be a pretty stiff price to pay for a prestige objective, especially when we know that we've got to pull back and let the other fellow take over.'

The Supreme Commander did not comment. He finished the conversation with a few unimportant words, but as a preoccupied Bradley put down his telephone he felt he had made his attitude to the subject pretty clear. Now it was up to Eisenhower.

Bradley need not have feared. On the following day, Saturday the 14th, Eisenhower worked out his plans which he would cable to the Joint Chiefs-of-Staff in Washington that evening. They were clear and unequivocal. As he saw it the enemy would attempt to hold out in two places only—the feared 'National Redoubt', the mountainous area of Bavaria and Upper Austria, and in the north around Bremen, Hamburg and reaching up the Schleswig-Holstein peninsula. As a result he planned to throw Patton's 3rd Army and General Devers' 6th Army Group southwards into the Bavaria–Austria area and Montgomery's 21st Army Group across the Elbe to secure Hamburg and to drive for Lübeck on the Baltic.

It would, he felt, also be desirable 'to make a thrust to Berlin as the enemy may group forces around his capital and, in any event, its fall would greatly affect the morale of the enemy and that of our own peoples'. But the drive to Berlin would have to take 'low priority in point of time unless operations to clear our flanks proceed with unexpected rapidity'.

In essence, therefore, his strategy for the rest of the campaign in Europe was threefold: to establish a firm line on the

5. According to Cornelius Ryan, who interviewed Gen. Bradley on this subject for his *The Last Battle*, the latter stated: 'Certainly I did not expect to suffer 100,000 casualties driving from there (the Elbe) to Berlin . . . It was in Berlin, as I saw it, that we would have suffered the greatest losses.'

western bank of the River Elbe; to allow Montgomery to launch his attack over the Elbe towards the Baltic between Lübeck and Wismar; and finally to start a powerful two army thrust southwards into Bavaria–Austria. As a consequence, *'Since the thrust on Berlin must await the outcome of the first three above, I do not include it as a part of my plan.'*

Bradley had won.

## IX

On Sunday morning after a day of bitter fighting on the Elbe in which General Hinds' CCB had been forced to withdraw from their bridgehead across the river—the first time the 'Hell on Wheels' Division had been forced to retreat in thirty-six months of combat in Africa and Europe—General Simpson received a telephone call from Bradley at the latter's headquarters at Wiesbaden.

'I've got something very important to tell you,' he told a mystified Big Simp, 'and I don't want to say it on the phone.' He then ordered Simpson to fly immediately to Wiesbaden. An hour or two later Bradley was waiting for him at the airfield just north of the town, still littered with the wreckage of Focke-Wulfs and Heinkels, as he stepped out of his plane.

Simpson saluted and they shook hands with surprising formality. Bradley did not pull his punches. Now he knew that all his plans were running smoothly, he did not want to waste time on this moment of unpleasantness with Simpson. 'You must stop on the Elbe,' he said baldly. 'You are not to advance any further in the direction of Berlin. I'm sorry, Simp, but there it is.'

'Where in the hell did you get this?' he demanded.

Bradley looked at him coldly from behind his steel-rimmed glasses. 'From Ike,' he said simply.

Simpson was too stunned to remember much of what was said after that. 'All I could remember,' as he recalled later, 'was that I was heartbroken and I got back on the plane in a kind of daze.'

As the plane flew over the war-torn countryside, heading north-east, all he could think of was: 'How am I going to tell my staff, my corps commanders and my troops? Above all, how am I going to tell my troops?'

When he arrived at his HQ he had composed himself somewhat. There he told the correspondents attached to his army

30

who had been alerted that something was afoot by his sudden disappearance, 'Well, gentlemen, here's what's happened. I got orders to stop where we are. I cannot go to Berlin.'

There was a murmur of sympathy and surprise from the correspondents. 'That's a hell of a shame, sir!' one of them said.

Simpson concealed his mood. 'These are my orders,' he said grimly, 'and I have no further comments to make.'

To take his mind off the terrible disappointment he left for the Elbe, after telling his corps commanders what had happened, to visit the 2nd Armoured Division HQ. Here he bumped into an almost exhausted Brigadier-General Sidney Hinds who the day before had seen the cable of a cable ferry he had built across the river snapped by an unbelievable million-to-one shot from a German artillery piece. He looked at his boss, worried that Simpson might be angry at his slow progress across the Elbe. 'I guess we're all right now, General,' he said. 'We had two good withdrawals. There was no excitement and no panic and our Barby crossings are going good.'[6]

'Fine,' Simpson said. 'Keep some of your men on the east bank if you want to.'

Hinds looked at him puzzled.

Then Simpson explained: 'But they're not to go any further. This is as far as we're going.'

Hinds looked at him shocked. 'No, sir,' he replied. 'That's not right. We're going to Berlin.'

As Hinds recalls, Simpson seemed to struggle to control his emotions. Then he spoke in a flat, dead voice: 'No,' he said, 'we're not going to Berlin, Sid. This is the end of the war for us.'

Now the River Elbe and what lay beyond would be left to the British Army and Field-Marshal Montgomery.

6. By Sunday the 2nd was using the 83rd Division's bridgehead there.

# 2

# The Assault on Bremen
## 15–26 APRIL, 1945

'Come on, you lucky buggers, I've got a lovely battle for you.'

*XXX Corps Brigadier to his staff,*
*1 April, 1945*

I

The Germans came for the last time at dawn on 15 April. At five o'clock in the morning, just as it was beginning to get light the rumble of the artillery, the ever-present background music to the war, started to rise in volume. Far away to the rear the 'heavies' coughed into action. The 88s joined in, tearing the dawn apart with their flat, ripping sound. A 'moanie Minnie'—the dreaded six-barrelled mortar—added its stomach-churning howl to the thunderous cacophony. Machine-guns began to chatter.

In their foxholes the men of the 1st Worcestershire Regiment waited expectantly. But it was not long before the fire wave came down on their positions along the bank of the River Lethe. Air bursts exploded in violent balls of red and yellow above their heads. Soil showered them. Scalpel-sharp shell splinters swept through the air. Men screamed out in pain. Here and there a man slumped to the wet bottom of his hole, dead.

The bombardment lasted exactly five minutes. Then it stopped abruptly, leaving behind a loud echoing silence. Cautiously the Worcesters raised themselves from the bottom of the holes. Shaking the mud and rubble away, they peered over the tops of their slit trenches. NCOs asked for reports of casualties. Officers shouted for them to 'stand to'. Rifle bolts were checked; hand grenades were placed on the top of the trenches; Bren magazines clamped open; safety catches released. *The Jerries were coming!*

They came down the hill to the north-west—200 of them or more. To their front were two Mark IV tanks, their structures camouflaged by branches and netting, their long cannon swinging slightly from right to left, like the snouts of predatory monsters seeking out their prey. Behind them came the foot-weary infantry in two long grey lines. They picked their way slowly, holding their machine-pistols and rifles across their bodies or at their hips. Here and there an officer opened his mouth and shouted to the men following him, but against the rattle of the tank tracks the Worcesters could not make anything out of the orders.

There was silence now in the British line, save for the heavy breathing of the waiting men, crouched in their trenches like a line of moles. Then a German officer blew his whistle. The tanks opened up with their machine-guns, sending a stream of red and white tracer forward. Men ducked instinctively. Lead pattered among the trees behind them. The tanks increased their speed. The infantry bunched themselves into two tails behind them. Officers waved their pistols. Here and there a man began to fire towards the Worcesters.

Suddenly the British line erupted into violent action. Brens started to chatter. With a clicking of bolts, the riflemen went into action. Officers stood up and taking deliberate aim with their 38s, shot in the direction of the advancing grey line, knowing full well their bullets wouldn't carry more than 100 yards. The Germans came on.

Then they were in the slit-trench line. Desperate little fights broke out everywhere. Men swayed back and forth on the parapets, cursing and groaning, sweating violently with the exertion of killing each other. A Company's two forward platoons were overrun. Lieutenant Smith, their platoon leader, fell dead in the mud. The Germans pressed on. D Company's right flank crumbled and broke. Here and there a Worcester, his eyes wide and blank with fear, started to scramble out of his hole and run to the shelter of the trees to the rear. Desperately Lieutenant Crossingham rallied what was left of D Company and fought back. The Germans faltered. For one moment Lieutenant Crossingham thought they had had enough. But he was wrong. Their young officers, hardened by the bitter battles of the Eastern Front, brooked no hesitation. Waving their machine-pistols, they ran forward over the shell-broken ground calling their men to follow them.

For two hours the battle raged in the woods that lined the River Lethe's banks, but the Germans simply could not penetrate the defences of Major Hall's A Company. Their dead and dying lay in bloody heaps everywhere. 'Sanitaeter!' their wounded called pathetically, but no stretcher-bearers came.

The 'stubble-hoppers', as the German infantry called themselves cynically, began to fall back. But they did not run. Doggedly they fought for every metre of German earth that they had to give up. The woods echoed with the chatter of their machine-guns as they withdrew. Yet as the hours passed, the chatter grew fainter and fainter, till it disappeared altogether. They were beaten. On that April morning they had made their last attack of the war on the 43rd Infantry Division.

As the Worcesters of the 43rd started to advance again that same afternoon, timid old men and women emerged hesitantly from the woods. Humbly, with the aid of dumb show and signs, they asked the officers if they could take away the German dead on the little handcarts they had brought with them. The officers gave their approval. With sorrowful faces the old people in their shabby black clothes moved slowly among the dead, sprawled in the grotesque postures of those killed violently in battle.

Many of the dead were boys, eighteen- and nineteen-year-olds, clad in camouflaged jackets, given a machine-pistol and thrown into battle; others were in their late forties—the last scrapings of the barrel. Now they lay there in the muddy field, young and old, their limbs already growing rigid. As they moved among them, lifting and carrying, their black aprons stained with blood, the old men and women were crying. It was a sombre scene, 'pathetic in its utter futility', as one eyewitness remembers, 'even to the battle-hardened troops of the Division'.

But now the chase was on and the troops of the British 43rd Division had little time to reflect upon the futility of war. As dusk came on that Sunday, the Somerset Light Infantry, taking over from the Worcesters, and supported by the tanks of the 13th/18th Hussars, started their final assault on the small German town of Ahlhorn. Covering their attack with smoke they crossed their start-line and swung into action.

The lead platoons advanced across the damp flat North German fields. Before them lay the positions held by the enemy, crouching unseen in their narrow sandy pits between the silver trunks of the birch trees. The Germans waited behind the thin, perforated barrels of their *Spandau* machine-guns.

Then the old ritual of death that the infantry had come to know so well since Normandy began. The machine-guns started their song of death. Men fell heavily into the grass. Exploding shells flung up great brown pillars of smoke. Mud

34

and muck showered the advancing men. Great holes appeared in the field. But the infantry went on.

Now the first of them were among the Germans. Where the enemy was too slow to raise his hands and yell '*Kamerad*', he got a kick in the stomach or a rifle butt to the face. But resistance was weak and within an hour the Somersets had taken forty prisoners including two immaculate, bemedalled *Luftwaffe* officers.

They pressed on into Ahlhorn itself. Sergeant Carroll of 7th Platoon, leading the way, fought on to the telephone exchange. As he stood panting at the door, his eye fell on the switchboard, still intact in the chaos of the hurriedly abandoned exchange. In its centre there were two sockets. One was labelled 'Bremen' and it was still plugged in. Sergeant Carroll hesitated. Was it a booby trap? Then he walked slowly and carefully over the paper-littered floor and thrust in the other socket. Drawing a deep breath, he summoned up his total German vocabulary.

'*Wer da, bitte?*' he said hoarsely into the mouthpiece.

Very faintly, but still distinctly, a female voice answered, '*Hier ist Bremen.*'

Montgomery's army had reached its objective.

## II

On the day that his armies reached the outskirts of Bremen, which he knew he must take before he could launch his men across the Elbe, Montgomery and his tiny tactical staff were as usual in the middle of nowhere. Unlike Eisenhower or Bradley or Patton, Montgomery did not like the large headquarters, set up in some large requisitioned building, preferably a castle or château, complete with hundreds of staff officers and servants. He preferred to set up the handful of caravans and headquarter cars, which he called 'home', in some German field close to the edge of a wood for camouflage purposes and operate from there with the aid of a few choice staff officers and his dozen or so 'eyes and ears' under the command of Major Poston of the 11th Hussars.[1]

He did not like the atmosphere of the big headquarters,

1. The 'eyes and ears' were young American and British officers, all in their twenties and battle-experienced, who daily drove out to the various fronts and brought up-to-date news back to him personally.

especially Eisenhower's with its 5,000 staff and male and female hangers-on. He preferred a small group of totally male company, to whom he could talk with the utmost frankness at the evening 'chats' before he drank his nightly glass of warm milk and turned in punctually at ten o'clock. He was especially glad of the smallness of his TAC HQ this April; it helped him overcome his rage and disappointment at the turn of events.

Seven months before, Eisenhower, then completely dependent upon the experience and know-how of the victor of El Alamein, had written to him that 'Clearly, Berlin is the main prize'. Since that time a lot of water had flown under the bridge, but in spite of his ups and downs with Eisenhower he had still firmly believed that one day he would lead his armies to the German capital. Then on 31 March he had received a message from the Supreme Commander which had dashed his hopes to the ground. It had read in part: 'You will note that in none of this do I mention Berlin. That place has become, so far as I am concerned, nothing but a geographic location, and I have never been interested in these. My purpose is to destroy the enemy's forces and his powers to resist.'

As Montgomery saw it now, 'the important point was ... to ensure that we should have a political balance in Europe which would help us, the Western nations to win the peace. That meant getting possession of certain political centres in Europe before the Russians—notably Vienna, Prague and Berlin.'

But now he knew that 'it was useless for me to pursue the matter further'. He had his assignment and he would carry it out to the best of his ability, but it went against the grain to concern himself with the drive to Bremen and then on over the Elbe, when he felt he should now be planning the last thrust to Berlin. Still he had his orders, but did he have enough men to carry them out? For not only were his three corps in Germany expected to capture the country's two largest ports, Bremen and Hamburg, which would eat up his infantry if house-to-house combat started and where his armour and air force would be of no avail, but they were also expected to cross the country's last great water barrier, the Elbe, and 'offer a firm front to the Russian endeavours to get up into Denmark and thus control the entrance to the Baltic.'

It could be done, he reasoned, but in order to speed up the advance he would have to make his divisions operate 'in great depth on narrow thrust lines', which was a risky business. Sitting there in his caravan staring at the portrait of his latest opponent Field-Marshal von Rundstedt,[2] he glowered at the thought of Simpson's army, which had been under his command until two weeks before, sitting on the Elbe doing nothing.

Every war produces its own heroes. But it had taken three years of defeat after defeat before the little hook-nosed general in his fifties had made his appearance in 1942, won his first victory and placed his own particular imprint on the conduct of Britain's war from then onwards.

Bernard Law Montgomery, the Bishop's son who neither drank nor smoked, whose wife had died years before, was a different kind of general from the bemedalled, glittering, red-faced general officers that the British were accustomed to. He was small (5′ 8″) skinny (144 lb) and was decidedly careless about his dress.[3] Indeed he often affected an odd mixture of civilian and military clothing, and more than once he had made public appearances carrying a ragged old 'gamp'—an umbrella.

Montgomery talked to his men in a manner quite unlike that of so many of his fellow-generals who had grown up in a military environment where that 'sort of thing' had been left to the NCOs; and where if they had come from the 'Brigade' (as they always called the Guards) the private soldier had stared woodenly ahead in the presence of an officer and asked for 'permission to speak, *sir*!' He talked to his men, told them what he expected them to do and promised them that they would never be involved in any of those great blood-lettings that had so embittered him about the generals of World War I; for Monty there would never be another Somme.

Yet there was still plenty of the upper-class Britisher about Montgomery. He had trouble with his 'r's, making them sound like 'w's as did so many products of the 'great' public schools. His outlook was still dominated by that legacy from the British imperial past which maintained there was only one way of life and that was the British one; as a consequence everything 'foreign' might be interesting or even quaint, but it was 'decidedly not British' and therefore wrong.

It was an outlook and an attitude that did not endear Montgomery to his American colleagues, especially as it was compounded by his ascetic teetotalism and those conferences at

2. In Africa he had started the habit of placing a picture of his current opponent in his caravan so that he could look at the man and try to assess how he might react.

3. The King had even chided him about his 'sloppy' appearance.

Montgomery's HQ which began with the standard opening, 'You will have exactly thirty seconds in which to cough, gentlemen.' In spite of their first name basis they could never get close to the outspoken Britisher with his holier-than-thou manner which riled them so often. As a consequence they drew back, retreated into their own rugged Americanism; and began to look for the chinks in the armour of this strange, bird-like little Englishman, with his funny hats and even funnier attitudes.

And over the winter of 1944–5 they found it: the 'Field-Marshal', as Patton called him contemptuously after Montgomery's promotion in September, 1944, was continually fighting the 2nd Battle of Alamein over and over again. His famous victory in the desert had had a traumatic effect on him and had become an obsession, as events in the post-war world would show.[4] Every battle he fought thereafter, with the notable exception of Arnhem, would be another Alamein with its massive build-up until with the tremendous resources of manpower, armour, artillery and air power at his disposal *he knew he simply could not lose.*

But now on this wet April day, planning his last drive to the port city of Bremen and then on to the Baltic, Montgomery must have realized that for the first time since El Alamein he no longer possessed the overwhelming weight of equipment and number of men he was accustomed to. He no longer had Simpson's seventeen divisions at his disposal; he would have to make do with the British 2nd Army and 'that article', as his great predecessor Wellington had once called the British soldier.

III

In that second week of April the rapid drive of the British 2nd Army from its Rhine bridgeheads came to a virtual halt while Montgomery 'regrouped'—one of his favourite expressions—'tidied up' and prepared for another El Alamein at Bremen.

Everywhere the vehicles of Horrocks' 100,000-man strong XXX Corps which would have the job of attacking the port-city crowded the tiny cobbled roads of the frontline area: a confusion of Humber staff cars, White infantry half-tracks,

4. The post-war El Alamein reunions in London were an example.

Dingo scout cars, Sherman and Churchill tanks, Bren and Lloyd carriers, three-ton trucks and 50-foot pontoon tractors— a great mass of olive-painted machinery, with the white star of the British Liberation Army the only spot of colour, clogging every road, farm track and field, and all pointing one way— North to Bremen.

And now the Tommies waited and prepared for what was soon to come. Some of them belonged to divisions with a long and glorious tradition behind them such as the 3rd Infantry Division, with its black and red triangle divisional sign; a good assault division, which had once been commanded by Montgomery himself, and which had fought its way from the Normandy beaches to the River Weser. Others belonged to less successful formations such as the 43rd 'Wessex': an unlucky division which had suffered greater casualties than any other— some 12,500 in the last year. Some were relatively new to combat. One such was the 52nd Lowland Scottish, the Army's largest infantry division, reckoned by the Corps Commander, Brian Horrocks, to be his best because of its high percentage of well-trained personnel.

While they waited, the British soldiers made themselves comfortable in the villages and big brick, half-timbered North German farmhouses where both humans and animals slept under the same dark thatched roof and the whole house smelled of animal droppings and boiled white cabbage. The Tommy liked his comfort, He did not like to be hurried. There was always time for a 'brew-up'—and every British infantryman went into action with a white or brown tea-mug hanging incongruously from the straps of his combat pack.

Now they bedded down under the thick German feather-filled *Steppdecken*,[5] looted the local farmer's eggs in the morning or swapped them for the ubiquitous 'bully beef' or 'M & V (meat and vegetable) Stew', and looked forward to their treasured daily one slice of bread and the evening issues of half a mug of government rum (though those who were motorized were already lugging around huge 50-litre carboys of looted German gin with them. Drunkenness was soon to become a problem in some battalions.).

But on the whole they were quiet, well-behaved, unaggressive men (except for some of Horrocks' Scotch infantry recruited from the slums of Edinburgh and Glasgow, brought up in the environment of gang fights of the depressed, bitter thirties), who were not rated very highly as offensive troops by

5. Eiderdowns.

their German opponents. At Arnhem, General Bittrich, Commander of the II SS Panzer Corps, had said of them to his staff: 'We must remember that British soldiers do not act on their own initiative when they are fighting in a town and when it consequently becomes difficult for officers to exercise control. They are amazing in defence, but we need not be afraid of their capabilities in attack.' By nature the 'squaddie', as they often called themselves, moved slowly and at a deliberate pace, doing only what was ordered of them—no more, no less.

But how should they be otherwise? The whole spirit of the 2nd Army was conditioned by the El Alamein obsession of its Commander-in-Chief and his concern for a slowly built up, 'tidy', controlled 'set-piece battle'. It was an attitude not improved by the quality of the officers who led them into battle; for—apart from certain notable exceptions—they were, at the best, amateurs, brought up in that public school tradition which despised the professional and saw something admirable and decidedly gentlemanlike in 'muddling through'—or as they often put it with pride 'making an absolute balls-up of things'. It was not without significance that to 'talk shop' in their messes and clubs meant that the 'culprit' would have to pay for a round of drinks. Even in the midst of war they cultivated their class habits. While Horrocks' unfashionable county infantry regiments bled to death in the *Reichswald* battles that winter, Guards officers noted in their memoirs that the oysters and whitebait from the Scheldt filled a gap in the gastronomic world, the latter, however, being rather a deceptive fish since 'they refused to produce any results when fried in the English manner' and that 'a certain restaurant in the Belgian town of Diest' had a 'cuisine which equalled anything that Brussels could offer', and in addition, 'had a pleasantly personal note that some of the smarter places lacked'.

Their conception of war was that it was a rather lethal form of sport. They rarely 'advanced' with their tanks; they had a 'gallop forward'. Their spells in the line were regarded as a 'jolly good—or bad—innings', and if prisoners were taken, the latter were a 'decidedly good bag'. In some of the 'better' regiments, 'game books' were kept of the officers' personal scores in Germans killed and certain sections of the front were described as possessing *excellent rough shooting*.

These products of the public school system, who felt that it was their birthright automatically to command (if they ever thought about the subject), tried to maintain the class barrier even in the mud and blood of the line. Guards officers insisted that their men approach them with the traditional 'permission

1 *Major-General Miles Dempsey who commanded the 42nd Armoured Division.*  2 *Major-General James Gavin, Commander of the US 88th Airborne Division*

3 *Lieutenant-General George S. Patton, Commander of the 3rd US Army; Lieutenant-General Omar N. Bradley, Commander of the 12th US Army Group, and General Sir Bernard Montgomery, Commander of the Allied Ground Forces in France, discuss the progress of the French campaign somewhere in France.*

4 *The reason for the Germans' hysterical fear of the Russians and their determination to fight them to the last. A Goebbels propaganda photograph taken in a recaptured German village after the Russians had been driven out.*

to speak, sir' before they would deign to answer; and even in the county regiments, most dealings with the 'other ranks' were carried out through the NCOs. Unlike the American or even the German Army under combat conditions, messing was separate. Every officer, even the most junior, had his personal batman, who produced the 'morning tea' and shaving water for 'his officer' and ensured that the latter's kit was always kept in order and 'laid out'.

These officers believed that the British solder was a simple soul, content as long as he had his beer, football, 'fags' (fifty a week, free issue in the line, along with a tin of sweets and a couple of bars of bitter, blue-wrapped chocolate), who could always outmatch his enemy as long as he could perform the intricate, three hundred-year-old drill movements of the British Army; for wasn't he led by gentlemen, who had had it bred into them in their public schools that they were born to lead—and win?

Thus in that second week of April, 1945, Horrocks' Corps waited, drinking its compo tea[6] and rum, eating its corned beef and looted fried eggs, smoking its 'coffin nails' (as it called its favourite cigarette, the Woodbine), cleaning its weapons— and its boots too. For the last time in World War II (and although they did not know it then) perhaps for the last time in history, a major British Army prepared to go into battle.

IV

But if his men were sanguine in that phlegmatic, plodding British way of theirs, their commander, Brian Horrocks (known to his men as 'Jorrocks') did not like the prospect of a set-piece battle for Bremen one bit. The tall lean general with a beak of a nose which dominated an ascetic, almost ecclesiastical, face had tried to sell the job of attacking the port-city to his neighbour Neil Ritchie, who commanded the British XII Corps. But as he noted regretfully, 'Now his corps was on the Elbe so there was nothing for it.'

But the more Horrocks studied the problem the less he liked it. He was faced with the task of attacking a great built-up area, defended by an admittedly mixed bag of troops, which would soon swallow up the four divisions of infantry at his disposal;

6. An instant powder tea, with sugar and milk ready mixed.

at the same time, both his flanks—in particular, the eastern one—were virtually unprotected against a surprise German counter-attack; and the recent attack on the Worcesters had shown the Germans were still capable of doing just that.

At the best his attack on Bremen could develop into an unpleasant miniature Stalingrad and at the worst it could be thrown completely off balance by even a regiment-sized German thrust from the East; and at this stage of the war he desperately wanted to avoid heavy casualties.

Taking advantage of Montgomery's halt to build up resources and supplies, he began examining the problem of Bremen in detail.

Before the war it had had a population of half a million and had been Germany's second greatest port after Hamburg, with which it had a common tradition going back to the illustrious times of the medieval Hansa merchants who had built the elegant patrician houses of the *Altstadt*—the old city. But in more recent times it had expanded across the River Weser, which ran now through the city, into the *Neustadt*—the new city—which had been transformed into a great industrial suburb, and which housed the huge concrete U-boat pens, the Focke-Wulf aircraft factory and the great Norddeutscher Lloyd shipping firm.

Now the city was reduced to an almost complete wreck. The years of British and American bombing had taken their toll. There were a few areas left where the high, terraced brick and stucco houses with their elegant iron-grill balconies, and the severely modern red-brick blocks of workers' flats built in the mid-thirties, were still intact. Elsewhere all was rubble.

Around the *Hauptbahnhof*, the main station, everything had gone; nothing was left save an intricate tangled mess of twisted girders and steel rails, with a girder bridge hanging limply into the River Weser. As one of the British air observers reported that week to the General: 'In the centre of the town, only the green leaden roofs of the Cathedral and the *Rathaus* stand, and in one part there is *nothing* to be seen above ground at all for a mile in any direction.'

So the green tower remained standing, like an accusing finger pointed at heaven—an ironical reminder to the Englishmen who had come to destroy the city that their forefathers had come from this very area and that an Englishman, St Willebad, had founded the Cathedral some twelve centuries before, becoming Bremen's patron saint.

But that April Brian Horrocks had no time for such philosophical reflections. His concern was the stone waste which faced him and the person of Lieutenant-General Becker, the Defence Commander of Bremen, his opponent. The tall bespectacled German commanded the remainder of the 1st Parachute Army, what was left of the *Horst Wessel Division*, the 18th SS Training Battalion (of brigade strength) and a hotchpotch of hurriedly thrown together units, made up of *Volkssturm*,[7] U-boat and motor-torpedo boat crews without boats and whatever else he could press into service.

It was a ragged force Becker had at his disposal, its heavy weapons limited to a few tanks, 88-mm cannon and flak guns. But it was a young force, stiffened with the fanaticism of a youth which knew only the teachings and readiness for self-sacrifice of the Hitler creed—one that would be prepared to fight to death. Horrocks had no illusions on that score.

Still his training and humanitarianism cried out against allowing Bremen to become a bloodbath at this late stage in the war when post-war Britain would need every able-bodied male it could muster (only a few months before Churchill had called up forty-five-year-olds for active service with the Army; the barrel, he knew, was scraped dry). As his 3rd and 51st Division approached the city he ordered leaflets to be fired into Bremen. They read: '*The choice is yours!* The British Army is lying outside Bremen, supported by the RAF, and is about to capture the city. There are two ways in which this can take place. Either by the employment of all means at the disposal of the Army and RAF or by the occupation of the town after unconditional surrender. The choice is yours as to which course is followed. Yours is the responsibility for the unnecessary bloodshed which will result if you choose the first way. Otherwise you must send an envoy under the protection of a white flag over to the British lines. You have twenty-four hours in which to decide . . .'

v

While Horrocks waited for the answer to his threat, General 'Bimbo' Barker, commanding VIII Corps, moved. Barker had once been fired by Montgomery in Italy and he was not risking the Field-Marshal's displeasure twice. He decided, while his two neighbouring corps regrouped, Horrocks in front of Bremen and Ritchie in the Hamburg area, that he would

7. The German Home Guard.

throw his corps forward to the Elbe. A few days before Montgomery had stated that he was going to 'bounce forward' to the river; he, Barker, was going to be the corps commander, he told himself, who was going to do the 'bouncing'.

For the job he picked his sole armoured division, the 11th Armoured which had come ashore in France completely unblooded but which had shown great elan and dash ever since, in particular in their race across Belgium to capture Antwerp; indeed they had outshone the 'Desert Rats' themselves, the 7th Armoured Division of Ritchie's Corps, who seemed to have lost the old 'get up and go' they once had in the desert. Starting on 18 April, the 11th Armoured was to reach the line of the Elbe between Winsen and Tespe on the morning of the following day.

Within twenty-four hours, the 11th had carried out Barker's hopes completely; they were on the Elbe. Then something happened with which the Division's commander General Roberts hadn't reckoned: intelligence reported that the unbelievable had happened. At the little river town of Lauenburg, a bridge was still standing! Admittedly it was a somewhat fragile railway bridge, which was not much use for heavy tanks. It would never be any good for an armoured division. But all the same—it was a bridge!

The General did not hesitate. His order went out at once, 'Get the Lauenburg bridge.'

Cautiously the Jocks of the King's Own Scottish Borderers edged their way through the little town of Sassendorf towards the bridge. It was still not quite daylight. But they could see their objective well enough: a long metallic structure spanning the river, disappearing into the town on the other side, merging into the little boatyard to the left and what looked like a small shunting station on the right.

Mostly they were small men, with bad teeth—the result of the bad nourishment of the unemployed thirties ('Gie's a packet o' chips, hinney'); and many of them were bandy-legged. They did not look much like soldiers, but they fought like an elite, in a bad-tempered vicious way which had gained them the nickname of the 'Ladies from Hell' in the First World War. If a German did not surrender quickly enough, he didn't get a second chance; and the official report would read 'No prisoners were taken'. The KOSBs were a tough regiment that did not subscribe to the nice 'fair play' traditions of the British home county battalions. They were ideal for the job on hand. In essence it was simple. While a tank battalion of the 11th Armoured waited to drive down the road from Hittbergen, they were to attempt to surprise the defenders of the bridge from the flank.

And the feint was coming off. Here and there a lone Jerry sniper spotted their shapes as they slid through the back streets like grey ghosts in the early morning mist, which wreathed their boots like smoke and muffled the sound of their progress.

By midday the Jocks had advanced to within sight of an embankment which covered the bridge on the near side of the river. But there they ran into trouble. Advancing cautiously in open order over the fields, the burr of a *Spandau* indicated that they had at last met firm opposition. A soldier pitched heavily to the ground and the rest dropped at once. A crackle of fire burst out along the line of an embankment.

The Jocks started to fire back, while their officers tried to estimate the opposition. It did not look good—perhaps a couple of hundred men and a single Tiger tank that added its 88-mm cannon to the rising crescendo of the battle. And even as its gun spoke, other German artillery from across the river opened up on the defenceless KOSBs in the open field. Hurriedly an officer called for artillery cover. The battle was on; the Germans now knew the British were after the Lauenburg railway bridge.

Gradually the British artillery's counter-fire brought the enemy across the river under control. One shell went wide, zoomed through the little town, penetrated the wall of the local museum and came to rest in the heart of a generously bewigged nobleman in a fading oil portrait which graced the museum's wall. The nobleman was George II of England, who in the later eighteenth century had also been ruler of this part of Germany.[8] The Jocks threw in a flank attack and the Tiger, scared that it might be put out of action by a British PIAT-man, the latter's clumsy primitive bazooka, scuttled backwards to safety. The defenders of the embankment began to follow.

Gradually the Jocks fought their way into Lauenburg, killing and taking prisoner nearly a hundred of the enemy. The tanks followed, urged on by Roberts' staff officers, their blood up now the bridge was within grabbing distance. By late afternoon the KOSBs controlled the eastern of the two railway lines leading up to their objective while the tanks had advanced to within 200 yards of the crossing and were swamping it with machine-gun and cannon fire.

Grimly taking and giving casualties the British got closer

8. For the curious, the portrait is still there, complete with hole.

45

and closer to their objective, advancing awkwardly and dangerously along the railway track and on both sides of the embankment over which it ran. Now through the haze and smoke of battle they could see the metal superstructure of the bridge quite clearly. An hour, their company commander promised himself, and it'll be ours. Opposition was now limited to small-arms fire; the Germans dared not use their artillery in case they hit their own men. It was clear that the opposition was weakening. Soon it would be all over bar the shouting.

Then tragedy struck. There was a sudden thick crump. The bridge shivered, rose slightly, and settled on its bed again. Next moment, there came a violent crack. A vivid sheet of purple flame split the evening sky. Timbers flew into the air. Girders followed. The Lauenburg railway bridge had been blown!

The Jocks stared aghast. Then their shoulders slumped, and the energy drained out of them as if someone had opened a tap. All their effort had been in vain. The last bridge across the River Elbe on the Anglo-American front had been destroyed. Now, once Horrocks had taken Bremen, the river would have to be taken by assault. The dash to the Baltic had suffered a serious setback.

VI

In London Mr Churchill was also worried by the failure of Montgomery's army to push eastwards with greater speed; but he was more worried that Thursday morning, the same day that the last Elbe bridge was destroyed, by Eisenhower's obstinate attitude on Berlin. Having received no reply to his letter to the new US President, he redoubled his efforts to change Eisenhower's mind.

As a result Ike had flown to London two days before and had been received with the pomp and circumstance that contrasted strongly with his first visit to the British capital three years before when his only reception committee had been 'Kay'—Kay Summersby, the British civilian driver who remained with him throughout the war, and who, through a complicated series of events ended as a captain in the US Army. Then he had been forced to go looking for the pretty redhead before she had whisked him off to Claridge's. That had been in 1942. Now he was received at 10 Downing Street by a beaming Churchill like visiting royalty.

46

But Churchill's beam hid his dissatisfaction with the American General, and as soon as the pleasantries were concluded he took the Supreme Commander to task for his lack of propriety in dealing directly with Stalin; it was an unheard breach of protocol, which he, Churchill, would never have tolerated from any of his generals, even from the 'insufferable Montgomery' as he sometimes called the head of 21st Army Group.

Boldly, a sure indication of Eisenhower's stature and the comforting knowledge that Marshall was in complete charge in Washington and backing him up to the hilt, the Supreme Commander stood his ground. He agreed that a better communications system should be established between the Russians and the Western Allies; but on purely military matters, which for him included the 28 March decision, he reserved the right to communicate directly with the Soviet dictator.

Churchill changed the subject to Berlin. Ike persisted in his belief that it was important to clear up his flanks first and then concern himself with Berlin. After all, he told Churchill, he had less than 50,000 men on the Elbe with little artillery at the moment; the Russians 15 miles closer than Simpson's 9th Army had two bridgeheads, 1,250,000 men and 22,000 pieces of artillery available for the job of capturing the enemy capital.

Churchill relapsed into silence and Eisenhower, who had a genuine affection for the 'Old Man', with his 'romantic' nineteenth-century ideas about war and the importance of one single battle for a whole nation's future, changed the subject.[9] As a concession to British pride, he began to emphasize the significance of Lübeck. Montgomery *must* take it—and soon— in order to keep the Russians out of the Danish Peninsula.

At first it seemed to the listening Churchill that Denmark was of little significance in comparison with Berlin, but slowly the American convinced him, especially as he kept stressing the huge forces available to the Russians for the attack on Berlin. Thus the meeting ended and a somewhat reassured Prime Minister walked with Eisenhower to the car in which waited Captain Butcher, formerly an executive of the Columbia Broadcasting Service and now Eisenhower's PR man and intimate. To 'Butch' the two of them looked as 'homey as neighbours on adjoining Iowa farms'. As the car sped away to Eisenhower's 'weekend retreat' Telegraph Cottage, some 25

9. Once Churchill had told Montgomery that his famous ancestor Marlborough had 'sat on his horse and directed by word of mouth a battle on a five- or six-mile front, which ended in a day and settled the fortunes of great nations, sometimes for years or generations to come'.

47

miles away from London through sordid bombed streets, where it had been only a matter of three weeks since the last V-2 had dropped, Ike relaxed. He told 'Butch' that the 'PM' always walked to the car with him—sometimes even in his bathrobe. He concluded that he had 'grown very fond of Churchill' and that although they occasionally differed on military operations, they were the 'best of friends'.

Then he closed his eyes and began to think out his message of that day to Marshall. Although all that afternoon he had defended his point of view that Berlin had no political importance yet contradictorily had stressed the urgency of not letting the Russians drive into Denmark, he was to write to his mentor a little later: 'I do not quite understand why the Prime Minister has been so determined to intermingle political and military considerations.'

On the day after Eisenhower returned to Rheims, Churchill sent an urgent cable to his Foreign Minister, Anthony Eden, who was in Washington.

'*For your eyes alone.*' it began. 'It would seem that the Western Allies are not immediately in a position to force their way into Berlin. The Russians have two and half millions troops on the sector of the front opposite that city' (for some reason he had inflated Eisenhower's figure). The Americans have only their spearheads, say twenty-five divisions, which are covering an immense front and are at many points engaged with the Germans.

'It is thought most important that Montgomery should take Lübeck as soon as possible and he has an additional American Army Corps to strengthen his movements if he requires it. Our arrival at Lübeck before our Russian friends from Stettin would save a lot of argument later on. There is no reason why the Russians should occupy Denmark, which is a country to be liberated and have its sovereignty restored. *Our position at Lübeck, if we get it, would be decisive in the matter.*'

Montgomery, the most political of the Allied generals on the Western Front, who could write that 'war is a political instrument; once it is clear that you are going to win, political considerations must influence its further course' was well aware of the issues involved in his drive to the Elbe and on to the Baltic. He had no illusions about 'our Russian friends from Stettin'; and he was determined to beat them to the sea. But there were problems. Where exactly were the Russians and what were their intentions?

All he knew, because of the complete lack of contact with the Soviet Allies, was that the Russian formation pressing westwards on his front was the 2nd Belorussian Army commanded by Marshal Konstantin Rokossovsky. The latter, he knew, was reputed to be a tough, handsome soldier with a weakness for women and wine who, in spite of the fact that Stalin had had him imprisoned in a concentration camp from 1937 to 1940, had remained a loyal supporter of the Russian dictator. In fact it was Rokossovsky who in 1941 had stopped the headlong German advance to Moscow. Thereafter his career had been a series of triumphs, which had reached its peak when he took the German surrender at Stalingrad.

A tough man and, as Montgomery was to find out three weeks later, a charming one with a sense of humour, as was revealed when Rokossovsky's envoy, sent to Mongomery's HQ to find out the Field-Marshal's tastes, was told that he did not like cigars, dancing girls or wine. 'He doesn't smoke and doesn't like women. *What the devil does he do all day?*' Rokossovsky demanded. In the light of the astonished comment, it was clear what the Soviet Marshal did.

But apart from a potted biography of the Russian Commander and a protest from the latter that elements of a British paratroop division were landing 'behind his back' (Rokossovsky told his staff the paratroopers were being used 'to plant border posts on German territory so that they—the British—could lay claim to it'), Montgomery's knowledge of the Russians was extremely limited. Yet his Intelligence had reported rumours that the Russians were landing parachute agents in Norway and Denmark to make contact with the communist resistance; and that Soviet torpedo boats had been reported off the East Danish islands. These were all signs that he must soon 'get cracking', to borrow one of his favourite phrases.

49

Studying the task before him, the all-out assault to capture not only the two major ports of Bremen and Hamburg but also, since the 19th, the necessity for a full-scale assault crossing of the Elbe, Montgomery came to the conclusion in his isolated little headquarters outside the medieval town of Lüneburg that he simply did not have enough strength to carry out the task.

Thus when Eisenhower came to see him on Friday, 20 April, to use his favourite piece of American slang he 'bellyached' to the Supreme Commander. Already in this campaign two of his infantry divisions had been forcedly broken up to provide reinforcements for the rest, whereas back in Britain Churchill had even been forced to call up skilled war workers to fill the ranks of his divisions depleted by the heavy fighting in the *Reichswald*. Eisenhower listened attentively. Then he promised to give him General Ridgway's XVIII Airborne Corps, once it had finished clearing the Ruhr Pocket. In addition, he approved of Montgomery's plan to capture Bremen first and then force the crossing of the Elbe, knowing Montgomery's horror of undertaking any task such as a river assault without massive preparation. All the same he warned him that Rokossovsky was making rapid progress through Mecklenburg on the other side of the Elbe, heading for the Baltic and Denmark. Once there nothing could stop them reaching the North Sea coast itself. Thereafter all that would be between them and the British Isles would be the North Sea.

The day after Montgomery received that salutory warning, Churchill received his long-awaited answer from the new US President. It was decided and firm—and utterly disappointing. Truman, who had already made it quite clear to his cabinet that he was to continue the policies worked out by Roosevelt, took the stand that the Western Allies must fulfil their commitments to the Russians, in spite of the latter's awkwardness. 'Our State Department,' he cabled to Churchill, 'believes that every effort should be made through the Allied Control Commission to obtain a fair interzonal distribution of food produced in Germany, but does not believe that the matter of retirement of our respective troops to our zonal frontiers should be used for such bargaining purposes.'

Churchill read through the long cable, until he came to the sentence which confirmed his growing realization that the new man in Washington firmly supported the Marshall principle that the strategy of the European campaign should be determined without regard to post-war political considerations. It read: 'The question of tactical deployment of American troops in Germany is a military one. It is my belief that General Eisenhower should be given certain latitude and discretion.'

Now Churchill knew that there was no hope of ever getting to Berlin; he would have to be content with sealing off the North Sea from the Russians and keeping them out of Denmark and Norway. That was up to Monty and his men.

VIII

On the evening of Sunday, 22 April, 'Bomber' Harris's Stirlings and Halifaxes, over 200 of them, swung in low over the almost defenceless port of Bremen. While the forward British artillery observers watched through their binoculars, 'Bomber' Harris's men went to work with a will. The earth shuddered and great dark fountains of dust and masonry shot up hundreds of feet into the sky.

At Achim, a village outside Bremen just captured by the infantry of the 52nd Division, an enterprising young officer found the railway telephone was still open to Bremen. He got the Bremen station-master on the phone. Hearing the bombers overhead, the frightening whine of their first 500-pounders coming down, he hastily offered to act as an intermediary with the German command.

Eagerly the young lieutenant, perhaps with dreams of promotion on his mind as a result of his initiative, waited for the man to come back to the phone. But before the station-master returned with his decision, the line went dead. It had been cut by the first bombs! So the slaughter of what was left of the defenceless port went on while its military commanders hid in their tall concrete bunkers in the fashionable *Bürgerpark* behind the burning main station.

Then at last it was over. An echoing silence descended upon the stricken port. Slowly the smoke cleared and the fires began to die down. But the forward observers could see no white flags waving. The uncompromising General Becker was determined to make a fight for it.

Reluctantly General Horrocks began to issue his orders. A large part of the city lay north of the River Weser and could most easily be attacked from the east. As his 52nd Division was already positioned on the Weser near the town of Verden, he decided that this division should attack along the east bank of

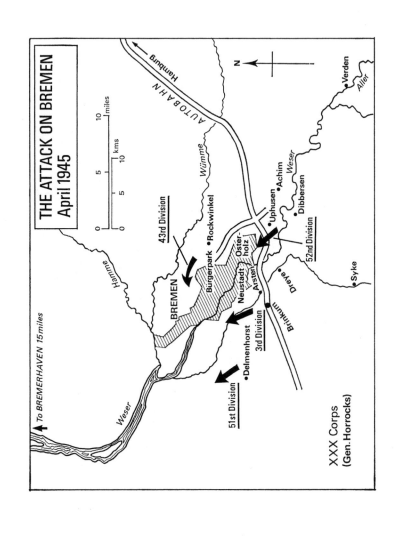

THE ATTACK ON BREMEN
April 1945

the river. To the 52nd's rear, the 43rd Division was to be held in readiness to intervene if necessary, especially if any German counter-attack developed.

On the south side of the Weser, he ordered the 3rd Infantry Division and the best known and most experienced of all his divisions, the 51st Scottish, known as the 'Highway Decorators' from their habit of plastering every town, bridge or hamlet captured by them with their divisional sign of the red 'HD', to continue their advance north-east in the general direction of Bremen and Delmenhorst. Thus as the dispatch riders hurried out with Horrocks' orders to the various commands, he had settled his mind on a two divisional thrust on each side of the Weser.

At midnight on 22 April the assault infantry of the 52nd Division in their camouflaged ski smocks began to take up their positions for the attack. It was pouring with rain. But as the Scots trudged through the miserable wet mire, with the rain dripping from the brims of their helmets, minds were on the morrow when the assault on Bremen would begin.

The assault started quietly enough. At four o'clock that morning A Company, King's Own Scottish Borderers of the 52nd Division, crossed their start line just outside the town of Uphusen. None of their company commanders had seen the ground in daylight and all that Major Andy Stewart of A Company had to guide him was an aerial photograph of the area. But in spite of the rain, the darkness and lack of reconnaissance, he confidently ordered his men out of their positions and began to lead them to their objective—a disused flak site. Behind them in reserve followed C Company. The night swallowed them up. As yet there was no noise of battle.

Within minutes they were out of touch. The area around Bremen was packed tight with gun batteries and various headquarters, all using more powerful radio sets than the '18' sets issued to the infantry. As a result infantry radio communication at company level was what the PBI called 'Piss-poor'. Anxiously the staff officers at KOSB HQ chain-smoked and waited for news. Time and time again they urged the radio operators in the little farmhouse lit by the hissing yellow glow of a coleman lantern 'to try again'. Now in the distance they could hear, dampened by the rain that came down in steady streams, the persistent rumble of their own heavy artillery intermingled with the crackle of small-arms fire and the high-pitched whirr of German machine-guns. There was obviously trouble somewhere, but where? It was almost daylight and still there was no news of the two lead KOSB companies.

Then abruptly the radios crackled into life. A Company came on the air. Thin but distinctly, distorted by the crackle of a hundred other sets. 'Three hundred yards short of objective ... wasn't deserted ... Jerry still occupying ... taking heavy spandau fire ... Intercepted a message from C Company ... Stating cut off to the rear...'

C Company was in a sticky position. Right from the start they had met heavy opposition, and they had been forced to take cover in a cluster of brown-painted wooden huts, During the night young SS troopers had sneaked in among their positions and dug in. Now the KOSBs were facing up to persistent Jerry attempts to blast them out of the huts with their *Panzerfausts*.

While the rain hit the shattered windows of the huts, flattened out and slid down like a thick wave of melted gelatine, the boys of the SS attacked with desperate courage. Running forward to within 10 yards of the huts, they would let fly with the bazookas, trying to blast holes in the walls before a rifle bullet or Bren burst would fling them to the ground.

As daylight broke, bursts of enemy machine-gun fire were tearing through the walls of C Company's HQ, the bullets ricocheting frighteningly around the room. Plaster flew everywhere. Fist-sized chunks of wood and brick whizzed through the air. Frantically the signallers tore up the floorboards with their jack-knives and buried their precious '18' sets in the holes. Something had to be done—and done quick!

Lieutenant Harry Atkinson, who had won the Military Medal as an other rank, volunteered to get help. Slipping out of the back door, he dashed across the open yard. Hardly had he gone a dozen yards than he was trapped by heavy small-arms fire. He dropped flat. Snipers spotted him. A slug struck the ground a couple of feet in front of his nose. Then another. Atkinson slumped forward as if hit. For fifteen minutes he lay absolutely still, flat in the mud, hardly daring to breath, knowing the snipers would be watching him through their telescopic sights. Then slipping off his pack, taking a huge gulp of air, he got up and made a desperate dash for safety, with his news.

At nine that morning Colonel Davidson, C.O. of the KOSBs, had a look at the situation himself. He didn't like it one bit. Swiftly he made his decision, The radios hummed. Shortly afterwards, the division's artillery cracked into action. The 25-

pounders poured shells down on the enemy positions, forcing the Germans to keep their heads down. Under their cover a troop of crocodiles[10] edged their way into the outskirts of Uphusen. Abruptly the artillery barrage lifted. For one long moment there was silence. Then a long stream of yellow and red flame shot from the muzzle of the first crocodile's cannon. It enveloped the first German-held house. From within came muffled screams. The occupants were seared by the flame. Their lungs collapsed from lack of oxygen. A crisp black parody of a human being appeared at an upper window, its flesh bubbling like the molten paint of the window. It screamed but no sound came from the burnt-away vocal chords. It dropped, mercifully dead.

The crocodile passed on. Behind it came the cheering Jocks. As an eyewitness records in the unfeeling prose of the time: 'The Jocks tore through the town pitching the Huns out of their holes at the end of the bayonet while the crocodiles roasted and the tanks blasted them out of the buildings. "B" Coy followed, yelling and cheering for all they were worth!'

By midday Uphusen was firmly in British hands. Bremen was now just three miles away.

IX

Major-General Thomas, the Commander of the 43rd Division, a tall, horsey-looking officer who invariably wore riding breeches and polished riding boots although he was an infantry commander, was now ordered to develop an attack on the great Hamburg–Bremen autobahn 6 miles north-east of Achim. After that was successfully completed he was to swing left and advance on Bremen along the road. The division found the going tough. The country roads along which they had to advance were narrow, cobbled and sandy-verged, and nicely salted with teller and anti-personnel mines. Casualties in vehicles and infantry were high as a result. But if the roads were dangerous, the fields were murderous. They turned out to be mostly reclaimed marshland in which tanks and heavy vehicles sank up to their axles, easy targets for fanatical youths armed with *Panzerfausts*. These sixteen-year-olds had developed a technique of fighting all their own. They would wait till some solitary vehicle, uncovered by infantry, was trapped,

10. Flame-throwing tanks.

trying to flail its way out of the mud. Then they would creep up with their one-shot bazookas and fire at point-blank range. Within seconds the vehicle would be turned into a roaring white-hot metal coffin; and they would be running for their lives, their faces wreathed with schoolboy grins, as if they had just placed a drawing pin on the chair of some unpopular teacher. But in spite of the terrain and the opposition, which in some places, according to the chroniclers, 'bordered on insanity', the 43rd pressed forward. They overcame the resistance of a party of well-entrenched sailors who fought bravely but who were facing the wrong way! They fought and beat a group of middle-aged civilian police armed with revolvers. They broke through a badly planned minefield. Then they hit the outer ring of flak guns which guarded the city against air raids and took six *Luftwaffehelferinnen*, female Air Force auxiliaries, prisoner.

The day before they had received a carefully worded and deadly serious GHQ pamphlet which had warned that 'Your attitude towards women is wrong in Germany. Do you know that German women have been trained to seduce you? Is it worth a knife in the back? A weapon can be concealed by women on the chest between the breasts, on the abdomen, on the upper leg, under the buttocks, in a muff, in a handbag, in a hood or coat ... How can you search a woman? The answer to that one is difficult. It may be your life at stake. You may find a weapon by forcing them to pull their dress tight against their bodies here and there. If it is a small object you are hunting for, you must have another woman to do the searching and to do it thoroughly in a private room.'

But as a 'private room' was not available on the battlefield, the infantry in the woods around Bremen were at a loss what to do with the women. In the light of the pamphlet everything and anything could be expected from their heavy-jowled grey-clad prisoners. But in the end the women were not searched and were treated with the utmost correctness. As one witness remembers—'they were just too damned plain!'

While the 43rd was having its headaches with its female prisoners, the 3rd—'the Iron Division', as it was called in World War I—prepared to attack from the south. There, two roads ran through flooded marshy fields to the villages of Dreye and Arsten and from there into the suburbs of Bremen. It was the Division's task to open up those two roads.

On the 24th, a day of sunshine and showers, the last preparations for the attack were made. Dozens of assault boats

5 *Admiral Doenitz with his adjutant; for three weeks, in 1945, Doenitz ran that part of Germany not under Allied occupation.*

6 *The attack on Bremen; infantry and tanks moving into Bremen, 25 April, 1945.*

7 *Prisoners marching out of the town after its capture.*

8 *German police watching the first British troops enter Hamburg, 3 May, 1945.*

9 *Men of the 1/5th Queen's Regiment moving through the centre of Hamburg after its surrender.*

and troop-carrying Buffaloes were brought up into the line. Everywhere the MPs were busy nailing up signs, indicating headquarters and marshalling areas. Yards of bridging and miles of white tape for marking routes through the minefields were piled up in readiness in the sodden fields. During the afternoon *Typhoons* swooped down on the village of Arsten, rockets shooting from their wings. Within a matter of seconds Arsten had disappeared in a cloud of dust and smoke. Towards evening the artillery barrage which had been falling on the doomed city all day, rose to a crescendo. And in the evening dusk the boxlike ambulances drove up and positioned themselves in the narrow lanes. Now their drivers chatted softly with one another, smoking a last cigarette, their eyes straying every now and again to the signs they had just placed in the front window of their vehicles: 'Attention, Carrying Casualties.'

It was almost time now.

At ten minutes to eleven that evening the artillery fire plan went into operation. Heavy fire drenched the German positions. All along the German lines the red flares began to soar into the sky. Green and white tracer stitched a flat pattern into the darkness. There was the crisp crackle of small arms. The battle was on.

At eleven three companies of the Somerset Light Infantry started to clatter along the road to Dreye. Captain Healey, commanding Y company, was hit almost immediately. He fell heavily and lay still. Captain Clapham rallied the leaderless company and led them towards their objective under intense fire. Major Read of Z Company followed, firing his carbine from the hip while his men roared their encouragement. Suddenly he realized he had used all his ammunition. Undaunted he ran on, using his carbine as a club when he stumbled into a German weapon pit. Moments later he was felled by a bullet which broke both his legs. His men rushed forward to help him. He refused it, though he was bleeding badly. Instead he lay where he had fallen, cheering his men on and calling on the Germans 'to come out and fight!'

While the wounded company commander encouraged his men, Private Wood of the Intelligence Section, took the lead, yelling at the enemy in German to surrender. It worked. They started to stumble out of their positions in droves, hands clasped at the backs of their heads, crying *'Kamerad'*.

By midnight the two villages of Arsten and Dreye were taken and the British were a little bit closer to drawing the noose tight around Bremen and strangling it to death.

Three days had passed since Horrocks had ordered the attack on the city, and he was worried. Admittedly his attack was successful all along the line, but time was running out and still his German opponent had not surrendered. And although Montgomery did not confide in any detail in his corps commanders, he knew that the crossing of the Elbe could not begin before he had captured the city. Thus on the morning of the 24th, he went out accompanied only by his driver, to view the 3rd Division's attack. Stopping his jeep he clambered up to the attic of a house, where two young artillery officers were bringing down fire on a group of German anti-tank guns which were holding up the 3rd's attack on a flooded airfield.

The two young officers glanced at the corps commander, who was wearing no visible badges of rank, failed to recognize him, and got on with their job of directing the 25-pounders.

For a few minutes Horrocks was able to 'forget the problems of a corps commander'. He lost himself in the front line duel taking place before him. The British artillery concentrations got nearer and nearer to the German positions. Suddenly it was all over. Smoke submerged the German anti-tank guns and when it cleared, their barrels were seen to be pointing drunkenly in the air. The young gunners who had directed the fire sprang to their feet and danced round the loft, crying: *'Got them! ... Got them ... a direct hit!'*

Silently Horrocks slipped out and left them with their joy. Somehow the episode had cleared his mind, filled him with renewed confidence that the damned port-city would soon be his.

One day later it seemed as if his confidence was going to be justified. At 19.30 Bomber Command launched a raid on the centre of the city. Visibility was good and the waiting British troops could see the planes distinctly.

Within minutes the whole central area was enshrouded by a pall of black smoke and dust rising thousands of feet into the air. Immediately the 52nd Division swung into action, taking advantage of the enemy's confusion. They attacked the southern edge of the city and sent the enemy reeling. They attacked all night and when dawn came, Harris's medium bombers came back and returned every thirty-five minutes, flying from fields in the Rhineland. They kept up the massive attack for five hours. Under the cover of this tremendous aerial bombardment the 52nd made rapid progress so that by the afternoon two of its brigades had penetrated 2 miles into the town between the main railway line and the River Weser.

Horrocks realized that the penetration completely changed the role of the 43rd Division. It could now, from its present positions, clear out Bremen east of the railway line which bisected the city. He knew that the railway line which passed through the southern end of the Bürgerpark[11] and threw off a branch line at Utbremer Vorst was the core of the city's defences. At the loop of this line and hidden in the park was a series of underground bunkers which housed the HQ of Major-General Sieber, Becker's subordinate and static defence commander, as well as the Guns Operation HQ of the Bremen anti-aircraft defence which was the basis of Becker's gun power.

Horrocks commanded General Thomas, commanding the 43rd, to attack the Bürgerpark at once. Its capture would deliver the *coup de grâce* to the German defence. The last act of the assault on Bremen had begun.

In bright sunshine on the morning of the 26th, the 4th and 5th Wiltshire Regiments left their start line at Rockwinkel and began to approach their objective. Advancing by a complicated system of leap-frogging a company at a time they took their first, second, third, fourth and fifth objectives without trouble. At seven-thirty the two lead companies raced ahead in their bren-gun carriers to take the sixth target. A road block of steel rails barricading one of the bridges across the autobahn brought them to an abrupt halt. As they flat-rolled out of their vehicles, expecting trouble, they found the barricade defended by two scared, long-haired boys armed with a lone machine-gun. The two heroes were, as one eyewitness put it, 'given a kick in the pants and sent packing', while the local populace were rounded up and ordered to pull down the barricade.

They pushed on. A huge seven-storey concrete flak tower barred the way. Its walls were protected by high blast barriers. It surrendered without a shot. Shaggy-haired, dirty prisoners streamed out in their scores. The vehicles moved on once more. A 20-mm gun started firing at them from a side road. The first shot put it out of action. Again they clattered on, leaving the gun's crew sprawled out around their weapon. The guards of a small concentration camp tried to put up a fight. They were put out of action within minutes. Roadblock after roadblock was rushed and captured. Nothing seemed able to stop the heady progress of the victorious Wiltshires. By late

11. A large park surrounded by pleasant town villas in white stucco nineteenth-century style.

afternoon they were within sight of their objective—the *Bürgerpark*.

Then the advance ran into trouble. As A Company entered the northern part of the park, heavy small arms fire swept their ranks from a German barracks in front of them. They began to take casualties. The company commander ordered them back. Hurriedly they sought cover in the doorways of the nearby houses. Major Colverson of the Wiltshire's C Company hurried forward to assess the situation. He was caught unawares as his carrier drove by the barracks. He slumped forward dead and the vehicle skidded crazily to a halt. Colonel Corbyn, who also hurried up to see what was going on, was felled minutes later and dropped to the concrete badly wounded. It was clear that the British troops were going to have a fight on their hands if they wanted the *Bürgerpark*. Generals Sieber and Becker were not about to surrender so easily.

While elsewhere in the wrecked city, littered by burned-out tramcars, telephone poles snapped off like matchsticks, piles of fresh brick rubble, the Germans were beginning to surrender everywhere to the infantry of the 3rd and 52nd Divisions, the 43rd fought a confused, bitter and bloody battle in the park. The Germans were well dug in among the trees and along the banks of the artificial waterways which dissected the park, and had entrenched themselves in the cellars of the villas.

By now the Wiltshire's attack had lost its steam. Thomas was forced to send in his reserve, the Somerset Light Infantry, plus two troops of the fearsome flame-throwing crocodile tanks, the final persuader in house-to-house fighting.

At last light on that day the Somersets, led by Major Watts, revolver in hand, launched their final attack. They advanced cautiously along the sides of a dirt road. Suddenly crackles of machine-gun fire swept along a line of trees to their front and the soldiers flung themselves into the dirt. '*Come on, lads!*' Watts bellowed and began to run forward. For one moment the men hesitated. Then the sergeants were on their feet pelting after their company commander. The men followed. The crocodiles lumbered into action. They clattered to within 50 or 60 yards of the enemy-held villas and fired. Screaming Germans, their clothes alight, rushed into the open where they were mown down by the Somersets. Burning houses cast a lurid light over the flame-throwers, as they waddled up the street 'flaming' one house after another.

Some time during the night Major Beckhurst of the Somersets met Major Pope of the Wiltshires. Together they stumbled on an enormous bunker situated in the centre of a grove of trees. With difficulty they found the entrance. Followed by a section of infantry with fixed bayonets they entered. Cautiously they made their way along the narrow, dim-lit corridors of the upper storey. All was utter confusion— discarded weapons, hundreds of pieces of paper, cans, ammunition everywhere—but completely deserted. They penetrated a lower floor. The place was a regular rabbit warren of staircases and small windowless rooms. Suddenly Major Beckhurst halted. He raised his hand in warning. Somewhere ahead in the gloom, voices could be heard! Beckhurst looked at Pope. What now?

Then the decision was made for them. A metal door creaked open and a drunken German officer, in one hand a champagne glass, in the other an empty bottle, staggered out and stopped abruptly when he saw the men in the corridor. For a moment his brain did not seem to appreciate the situation. Then his mouth fell open. The bottle dropped from his fingers and shattered on the concrete floor. *'Die Tommys sind da!'* he gasped.[12]

Swiftly Pope pushed him to one side. About thirty officers lay sprawled about a wooden table in the room. It was piled high with bottles of French champagne, while the corner was full of shattered 'dead soldiers' where the drunken officers had slung them. The Englishman gave an order. Slowly the Germans began to raise their hands. The two officers had captured the staff of Major-General Sieber. A few minutes later the static commander, an ancient and very stuffy warrior, joined his staff in their march into captivity. The end was very near now.

When dawn came the following morning the Wiltshire Regiment resumed its attack across the northern end of the park. Facing them was the last barrier, the canal. But the infantry were quick to improvise. Seizing the canoes of the Bremen Canoe Club, which lay conveniently near, they crossed the canal in style. D Company came under fire. Quickly the company commander made plans to assault the source of the trouble—a small barracks. But just as they were about to go in, a small group of Germans emerged, blinking their eyes in the thin morning light, waving a white flag. It was the staff of Major-General Becker. Becker was ready to give in. A little while later he emerged himself—a tall, amiable man, who had

12. The Tommies are here.

lost complete control of the confused battle and had been forced to direct what units he could contact over the civilian telephone system. The General was led away into captivity to join the 6,000 of his men who had surrendered with him.

In the cold rain which now began to fall, the city presented a picture of sordid horror. Its centre was blocked with great piles of brick and rubble. Lamp standards, twisted into impossible shapes by artillery fire, were silhouetted grotesquely against the leaden sky. Here and there ruptured gas mains added their stench to that of the shattered sanitation system. Everywhere thousands of slave labourers in their tattered uniforms with the word OST (for 'East') stencilled on their backs went on a wild orgy of looting, murder and rape. Breaking into the *Wehrmacht* supply dumps, they stuffed themselves with food and emptied the great 50-litre carboys of schnapps; and they danced and killed and copulated in the smouldering ruins of the once proud Hansa city of Bremen.

Working their way through the rubble and the drunken slave workers a patrol of the Somersets finally found the headquarters of the Nazi Party leader. But this time they did not make any arrests. As the door yielded under the blows of their rifle butts and they stumbled into the room, their brains reeled at the sight. Slumped over a table, which was bare save for an empty bottle of cognac, there was a woman, a bullet through her temple. Opposite her was her husband, the party leader, the blood congealed at his forehead, one hand still clutching the 9-mm pistol with which he had shot her and then committed suicide. The battle was over.

# 3

## The Attack at Artlenburg

### 27–30 APRIL, 1945

'He who holds northern Germany holds Germany.'
*General Blumentritt*

I

Field-Marshal Montgomery was angry. That morning, 27 April, he had received a report from the War Office that three days before Himmler had made an offer of capitulation to the West through the Swedish Count Bernadotte. Now as far as he was concerned 'the oncoming Russians were more dangerous than the stricken Germans'. He knew the 'German war was practically over' and that 'the essential and immediate task was to push on with all speed and get to the Baltic and there to form a flank facing east' against the Russians.

Sitting in his caravan outside the farmhouse of Farmer Knacke whose property in the village of Odeme near Lüneburg had been requisitioned the day before for Montgomery's HQ, he thought again of the messages with which both Churchill and Eisenhower had been bombarding him these last few days ever since the latter had convinced the Prime Minister of the importance of the Baltic. Already, according to the Supreme Commander, he should be ready to cross the Elbe, east of Hamburg.

Eisenhower's pressure exasperated him. Suddenly it seemed that the a-political American had become aware of the political considerations involved in this last campaign of the British Army in Europe. Abruptly it was all-important to Eisenhower that he beat the Russians to the Baltic. Did this mean that Churchill's and his urgent warnings were bearing fruit? If it did, then as far as he was concerned it was already too late. He simply did not have the strength to contain the Germans in Holland, push on to the North Sea from Bremen, take Hamburg and at the same time race the Russians to the Baltic. He had only Barker's four divisions to force the river and race the 68 kilometres to Lübeck; the Russians had 300,000 men for the same task!

As he sat and considered the problem his anger grew. While he sought frantically for strength to allow him to do the job Eisenhower demanded, Simpson's 9th Army, which had been taken away from him so suddenly and so unceremoniously on the 4th, was sitting on the Elbe fifty miles away doing absolutely nothing. With the American's force under his command he would double his present number of divisions. A month ago it had been his plan to use them for the last thrust to Berlin; now they were sitting idle and he did not even have enough strength to take his secondary objective—Lübeck.

He started to compose a letter to his boss in Rheims. He wrote (as he explained long afterwards), 'that I was well aware what had to be done but he must understand that when he had removed the 9th American Army from my command the tempo of operation slowed down automatically on the northern flank'. He concluded with the accusation that if he did not reach the Baltic coast before the Russians then it would be his, Eisenhower's fault.

We do not know Eisenhower's reaction when he received Montgomery's letter. But we do know that by now he had given up getting angry about the holier-than-thou attitude of the British soldier. He knew what Montgomery had to say was typical 'Monty bellyaching'. The latter viewed the Elbe crossing like he viewed all his major operations as something which had to be prepared for meticulously regardless of the enemy strength so that in the end he would have overwhelming superiority on his side.

Eisenhower read the letter through and told himself that by now Ridgway would have alerted his Airborne Corps to go to Monty's aid; perhaps that might keep the bad-tempered Field-Marshal off his back for a few days.

General James Gavin, Commander of the US 82nd Airborne, which was the backbone of the XVIII Airborne Corps received the news that his veteran formation was going to be in at the kill with relief, though the feeling was tinged with an underlying disappointment. Just over a month before he had assembled his staff close to midnight on Palm Sunday at his HQ in Sissonne, in France, to reveal to them the greatest assignment the division had received since North Africa. After checking security and telling the hand-picked officers present, 'nothing you hear tonight is to go beyond this room', he had pulled back the curtains covering the wall map.

'Gentlemen, we're going in for the kill. This is the Sunday

punch.' The staff officers had stared with open eyes at what the map revealed—*Berlin!* And, he had pointed out a little later, 'Our piece of real estate is right in Berlin itself—Tempelhof Airport.'

But the weeks had passed and nothing more was heard of the daring plan to drop two American and one British parachute divisions on the German capital. Gavin had grown nervous. As had his boss, General Ridgway, commander of the XVIII Airborne Corps, who in the first weeks of April had written confidently to 1st Airborne Army HQ: 'It is believed the reaction of the German mind will be tremendously influenced by the personal appearance of individual soldiers who participate in "Operation Eclipse".[1] It is the intention of this headquarters to take into "Eclipse" "A" dress as well as a field uniform.'

Class A uniform! Gavin had been forced to laugh when he thought of it, his mind full of the foreboding that he would be sitting out the rest of the war, doing nothing. As he was to write about the situation of his formation long after the war, 'About the kindest thing that one could say about that affair was that it was all very perplexing. Did Eisenhower really intend from the very beginning to carry out "Eclipse" and stop on the Elbe? Or did he intend to parachute into Berlin and seize it?'[2]

On 24 April, the Airborne Army had sent a cable to Eisenhower stating that it was 'assuming' that airborne operations to Berlin would not be required and requesting 'confirmation or clarification'. The Airborne HQ received its answer one day later. Eisenhower replied equally tersely: 'Airborne operations to Berlin under Eclipse conditions will not be required.'

1. The top secret allied plan to come into effect if it appeared that the German defences were about to collapse.

2. 'I since have gone into the matter quite thoroughly,' he wrote later, 'and about the only question remaining is—just how much information did Stalin have and when did he receive it? ... I am convinced that he knew by late February or early March of '45 that we were going to stop on the Elbe. His exchange of telegrams with Eisenhower, therefore, was something of a game.' Does this indicate a high-level spy in Washington or Eisenhower's or Bradley's HQs? Gen. Sir Kenneth Strong, Eisenhower's Chief-of-Intelligence, asked to comment on Gen. Gavin's remarks on the subject of Berlin, writes: 'It seems to me that Gavin is looking at 1944–5 events in the climate of present day Russo-American relations. In 1944–5 everybody was Russia's friend—except possibly Churchill.' As to the question of possible leaks or even spies at Supreme HQ or in Washington, Sir Kenneth feels the 'innuendo' has no foundation in fact.

Instead the Airborne Corps was going to be sent up the line to help Montgomery cross the Elbe.

II

On the banks of the Elbe, the British waited. On the whole Barker's 8th Corps front was quiet. For nearly a month his men had dashed across the flat North German plain. Time and time again, they had attacked enemy roadblocks, overcoming desperate German delaying actions at hamlets and villages whose names were only remembered because of the ghastly futility of the battles fought there. The miles had flown by. Twenty, thirty, forty a day! They would pull up at some forgotten village, looking with its medieval half-timbered cottages and turreted pseudo-Gothic nineteenth-century villas like a page from a child's colouring book. Laughing and joking they would drop heavily from their bren carriers and three-tonner trucks and clatter down the single cobbled street in their heavy ammo boots. Gleaming in the April sunshine would be the white bedsheets and towels—the Jerries were a clean people even in defeat—hung from every window; and every door would be neatly enscribed with the names of its occupants—as Allied Military Law required. Banging at the doors, they'd make eyes at the big-busted girls in their wooden shoes and skimpy flowered dresses: *'Fraulein, du schlafen mit mir?'* (a foolish question for they would be gone within the hour), search the rooms for German soldiers and loot the cellars of their hoards of schnapps and pickled eggs. Then they'd be gone. On to some new barricade. The chatter of a lone machine-gun. The crack of a six-pounder anti-tank gun. The crump of a 3-inch mortar. The clatter of heavy boots on the road. A voice crying *'Stretcher-bearer!'* The scream of pain among the firs. Within minutes it would be over and a few more khaki-clad figures would lie crumpled in the dust like broken dolls. The price of victory.

But now the rush was over. Before them stretched the broad expanse of the Elbe, the last water-barrier in the heart of Germany, and they, the infantrymen of the 15th Scottish Division, were to assault it. It would be their third river crossing of the campaign; for some of them it would be their last in both senses.

Together with the 1st Commando Brigade, the 15th Scottish were to play the major role in the first phase of the operation.

66

They were to assault the river between the fishing villages of Artlenburg and Avonsdorf and establish a bridgehead centred on the village of Schnakenbek on the other side. The bridgehead some 2,500 yards wide and 1,500 deep would be held, while Roberts' 11th Armoured passed through it on its drive to Lübeck and the coast.

Now in the last days of April, the Scottish infantrymen and the commandos to their right got down to the task of preparing themselves for the assault. The enemy wasn't aggressive. Indeed boatmen still plied their trade in no-man's-land, for the Elbe had become just that, in full view of both sides. Ferrymen offered to take the British across for twenty pfennigs or one cigarette, but the Glasgow infantrymen who held the bank on the British side suspected that the ancient Elbe sailors in their black, peaked caps and moleskin waistcoats were pulling their legs.

A British Commando officer tried to get Lauenburg to surrender on his own bat. But his boat's engine stalled in midstream and obliging enemy troops hauled him to safety to the other side, let him have a good insight into their defences but made no move to surrender.

And while they waited and watched, British observers could see German staff officers driving back and forth along the Lauenburg–Boizenburg road as if the enemy were 100 miles away. It all looked too easy.

Yet Barker and his planners knew that the crossing wasn't going to be a walk-over. At the point where the infantry would cross the Elbe, the river was 300 yards wide and the current ran at one and a half knots. It would take the amphibious vehicles of the 11th Royal Tanks, who were to ferry the infantry across, five minutes to do so; and in that time the enemy could bring his artillery to bear on slow-moving vehicles with disastrous results. They would be sitting ducks.

Even if the Royal Scots Fusiliers and Royal Scots who were to lead the assault got across without too many casualties, they still had to face sheer 100-foot cliffs, defended by an estimated eight or nine German battalions. As D-Day, 29 April, grew closer, Barker's planners, with the memory of Simpson's failure still fresh in their minds, began to worry more and more whether they could make it.

On the other side of the river Field-Marshal Busch, the overall German commander, was determined to see that they didn't. Once the British took the Elbe, he knew the whole German front on it must automatically collapse; and the

British would be in Hamburg in a matter of twenty-four hours.

It has been said since the war that Busch was a weakling who put up only a token resistance to the British. This is not true. The elderly German soldier was an exceedingly tough individual, who once in Russia when one of his staff officers had protested that German units were shooting Russian POWs outside his window had snapped laconically, 'Then pull the curtains.'

He had started the war well with successes in the French campaign, but in the middle years of the war in Russia he had lost much of his reputation and taken to drink. In March, 1945, the Führer, whose loyal servant he had always been, had called him back to the service after he had been without a command for nearly a year. Now, although his position on the Elbe was not exactly very good, it certainly was not hopeless. His men had plenty of fight in them still and Busch was out to rehabilitate himself in the only way he knew how—by fighting to the end.

Meanwhile back in the 15th Scottish's Headquarters at Scharnebek, planning went ahead, based on the assumption that the crossing must be a deliberate, carefully worked out affair which couldn't take place before 27 April.

In fact, the divisional staff came to the conclusion that the Elbe crossing would be even tougher than their Rhine assault a month before. There were only two approach roads to the crossing area—from Lüneburg to Artlenburg and from Scharnebek to the Lauenburg bridge (now blown). Between them the ground was marsh and bog so that the advance would be limited to these two roads. Unfortunately, too, the ground on the British side of the river was perfectly flat while on the opposite side it rose a hundred feet and was covered with thick fir plantations so that the enemy enjoyed a perfect view of the British lines to a depth of 6 miles. As a consequence they agreed that the 15th would not be allowed to move any vehicles by day and that the actual crossing would have to be a night one—a decidedly unpleasant prospect for both commanders and their men.

But the difficulties did not end there. Not only were they faced on the other side by the eight to nine battalions already mentioned, but they also had to contend with about a hundred flak guns used in the infantry role. In addition there was only one exit road from the bridgehead—the steeply winding, 20-foot-wide one that led out of Schnakenbek. This road would have to bear the major part of the 15th's traffic and that of the

11th Armoured as it began its dash to the coast. The Schnak-enbek road, the planners concluded, was going to be a definite headache.

There were further complications too. Colonel Foster, who was in charge of the Corps' engineers, would follow up the initial crossing by throwing a Bailey bridge and a raft ferry across the 300-foot-wide river. The Colonel would have to have these finished in time for the break-out; in fact the whole operation would stand or fall by the success or failure of Colonel Foster's bridging operations. Foster wondered what might happen if the Germans counter-attacked in strength? Or brought their artillery to bear on the bridge? Or threw in their last reserves of jet fighters and fighter-bombers which could easily outfly anything the RAF could put up to meet them?

While Colonel Foster and General Barber worried about the coming assault, the men of the infantry regiments relaxed. During the week's pause while the plans were worked out, reconnaissance parties from all battalions concerned visited the places where they would cross. Stealthily they made their way to the river at night and during the day remained concealed from the prying eyes on the cliffs of the opposite bank while they studied the ground. It was so peaceful by the riverside in that perfect spring that it was hard to associate the scene with the hard battle to come.

III

By Saturday, 28 April, D minus One, all was ready. Late that afternoon the long lines of trucks began to file into the marshalling areas. With them came the assault infantry. They were the best the Division still had alive. But in spite of the cocky angle of their flat helmets and their loud chatter they yawned a lot and relieved themselves a great deal—a sure sign of tension and nervousness.

But there was no going back. Given a hot meal—the last before the attack—they were told to bed down for a couple of hours. They were too nervous to sleep, though many of them had done this before on the Seine and Rhine. Here and there the more experienced changed into clean woollen underwear. If they were hit, the clean fabric that might be forced into the wound would be less likely to result in gangrene than if their underwear were dirty. Others methodically stripped their rifle

69

and bren magazines and sitting cross-legged in the grass, rubbed the shining brass cartridges before replacing them. Some tucked their issue metal shaving mirrors in their left-hand blouse pockets as a frail but sure means of protection for the heart; for they had all heard the wonderful story of a soldier in some other regiment—it was always in another regiment—who have been saved like this from a 'jerry bullet with his number on it'.

At eleven o'clock that night the Royal Scots and the Royal Scots Fusiliers filed on board the craft of the Royal Tanks. Again they were told to snatch a bit of sleep by busy staff officers who wanted the infantry quietly out of the way until the moment of assault. This time, however, sleep was out of the question even for the toughest of 'old sweats' among them.

One hour later the artillery batteries opened up and began blasting the German positions in a typical Montgomery 'Alamein barrage'. For the last time in World War II, British infantry in Europe were awed by the sight of a great barrage and the dramatic crimson fires that had begun everywhere on the other side of the river. The softening up had started.

At Artlenburg the sky was as bright as day in the light of the searchlights. And onlookers could stand unseen now in the shadows with nothing between them and the Elbe. Over the river a fantastic pattern of a myriad stabs and flashes of orange flame took shape and died, like man-made forked lightning. Here and there a maverick shell exploded close to the far bank and tossed up a ball of fire like a Roman candle. And all the while the tracer from the Bofors anti-aircraft guns passed in diagonal streams, throwing a crimson light on the water below.

The waiting infantry had no time for the terrible beauty of the sight. Their moment of truth had come. As 2 am approached, the air was filled with a droning roar like that of a squadron of heavy bombers. One by one, twenty-ton Buffaloes[3] swung out of Artlenburg's cobbled main street. They roared to left and right, fanning out along the river bank. Each had an appointed spot to cross. They lumbered up the 6-foot grass bank that separated them from the river, engines roaring in low gear. Then precisely at two, they waddled down the other side of the embankment. They splashed into the water like a school of hippos. Slowly they pushed out into the current. Almost immediately the British barrage rose from the

3. Amphibious armoured troop-carrying vehicles.

opposite shore to the top of the cliff. They were on their own now.

The Germans were not slow to take advantage of the respite. Bursts of machine-gun fire skimmed the water. Spurts of water flew up on all sides. The men crouched down, thankful for the protection of the thin metal sides. The Browning machine-guns of the Buffaloes chattered in reply. Here and there a man slumped to the floor of the craft. German artillery joined in. The enemy was nervous and his fire was inaccurate.

On the British side of the river, the Argylls and the KOSBs were waiting their turn to cross in a large quarry on the river bank upstream of Artlenburg. Suddenly they came under fire from German long-range guns. The men cowered against the soft white stone, arms clasped around their heads. A shell hit the entrance to the quarry which disappeared in a ball of crimson flame. Half a company dropped to the ground, dead and dying. Shaken but undaunted, the rest filed to the boats and prepared to cross.

The KOSBs followed. They made the crossing without incident, landing at Schnakenbek itself. They baled out of the boats and rushed the *Gasthaus* next to the ferry-station.[4] Green-clad German police from Hamburg tried to stop them but failed. The Jocks pushed relentlessly up the narrow exit road, leaving a trail of bodies behind them.

To the right of the 15th Division, the Commando Brigade had also made a successful crossing at Lauenburg. Now they faced a 150-foot cliff. But the green-bereted soldiers, who disdained the Army's steel helmet, were used to cliffs; they had trained throughout the war for such obstacles. Under the command of Captains Clapton and Cruden, they began to climb it, seemingly unaware that they had sixty pounds of equipment strapped to their backs in addition to their weapons and ammunition.

On the edge of the cliff the Germans leaned forward and lobbed potato masher stick-grenades at them. They exploded here, there and everywhere. Men screamed and fell off the cliff, to the tiny shingle beach below. But most of them kept on climbing. Then they were among the enemy. As Captain Clapton put it later in his somewhat terse report, 'the majority of the enemy in the immediate area were at once eliminated.'

An hour later the Commandos were regrouping at the edge

4. A quarter of a century later the ancient proprietress of the *Gasthaus* still talks with animation unusual in an eighty-two year old of that eventful night. She survived the burning of her inn, but her husband died of shock six weeks later.

of a sandpit to the north of Lauenburg, which the KOSB had failed to capture ten days before. As soon as dawn broke, they would launch an all-out attack on the town which, two hundred years before, had been British.

By dawn the situation was as follows. The leading troops had secured the immediate bridgehead and in the face of light infantry, but heavy artillery, fire were swinging left and right to their objectives. Meanwhile the 46th Brigade of the 15th, with the Cameronians and Glasgow Highlanders in the lead, was pushing through clear of the immediate bridgehead and advancing in a northerly direction on an 'advance-to-contact' mission. So far they had met little opposition.

Everything seemed to be going much better than planned. But Colonel Foster was worried as his engineers sweated and grunted at their bridge under continuous enemy shellfire. They were losing men steadily, but it wasn't the shellfire which worried Foster. It was unpleasant, but it wasn't the first time his men had worked under such conditions. It was the air attack that was his greatest fear. Over and over again his eyes scanned the horizon. Admittedly the RAF were trying to keep an umbrella of Spitfires over the bridgehead, but that wouldn't be much use once the Me. 262s got among them—the latter being at least two hundred miles an hour faster than the British planes.

The German jets came in at midday. A British tank officer remembers: 'The exit from the bridge was a steep muddy defile through the blazing village of Schnakenbek, and in consequence, there was a monumental traffic jam. I sat in my tank in the middle of the bridge for ages. The RAF had a remarkably efficient umbrella over the bridge, but while I was sitting there something went wrong and one lot of Spitfires went home before the next had arrived. In a second the Luftwaffe pounced: six jets in line astern screamed down on the bridge and plastered us with anti-personnel bombs. I felt very small, sitting in the open-top turret of my M10. With one continuous series of explosions and spouts of water they had dropped their load; it was over in a matter of seconds. They missed all of us sitting stuck on the bridge and were gone behind the trees. With an unsteady hand I lit a captured German cigar; I suppose I should have said to myself: 'Well, there opens a new chapter in man's achievement." But I don't think I did.'

Neither did Colonel Foster. By the end of the afternoon twenty-eight engineers had been killed or seriously wounded and the approaches to the bridge damaged. All day they kept coming in; and each time the squat streamlined black shapes howled away at an amazing speed, they left behind them more silent figures slumped awkwardly on the steel girders.

But worse was to come. Late that afternoon a section of Scottish infantrymen were patrolling the British bank of the river near the village of Tesperhude, when they were startled by two gleaming black shapes which emerged from the water. The section leader held up his hand. His patrol stopped automatically and looked open-mouthed at the two strange figures flip-flopping like semi-human fish in the shallows. The corporal fired a burst from his sten and the strange shapes halted abruptly. Slowly (as the report had it) 'they raised their flippers' in surrender.

When Foster heard of the capture of the German frogmen he knew the enemy would use everything they had to destroy his bridge—jets, floating mines, long-distance artillery, frogmen—the lot.[5]

On the afternoon of the 29th, General Gavin had just set up his Command Post further down the Elbe opposite the town of Bleckede when the big brass arrived—his Corps Commander General Ridgway and General Miles Dempsey, head of Montgomery's 2nd Army.

Gavin liked Dempsey. He had a scholarly mind and, unlike both Ridgway and Montgomery, who somehow both seemed a little retarded, had an entirely adult personality. He cared nothing for the newspaper publicity that so many generals lived for nor ever seemed aware that it was necessary for a soldier's career. Gavin felt much sympathy for him too, as he knew from his own experiences in the Battle of the Bulge what it was like to serve under Monty and what Bradley called his 'usurpation of authority'. Yet the 2nd Army Commander did not seem to mind Montgomery's constant interference in the running of his Army; Dempsey knew how to tolerate it without jealousy or anger. An excellent soldier, completely unknown to the general public—indeed even to his own men, he was, all the same, utterly loyal to his Commander-in-Chief.

On that warm April afternoon, with the wind from the north bringing the noise of the battle through the open window of Gavin's CP, he proved just how loyal he was. He knew and valued the aggressive ability of Gavin's airborne forma-

5. He needed not have feared. Although nearly forty jets were shot down over the bridge, it survived till 1947 when pack ice carried it away. Today the locals complain they still miss it; now they have to go to either Lauenburg or Geesthadt (both 10 miles away) if they want to cross the Elbe.

tion, just as he knew that his own men tended to the same careful pedestrian attitude as the C-in-C. Yet at the same time he had become aware that it was vital for the Allies to reach the Baltic before the Russians. Now he urged the Airborne Commander to cross the river during the night and establish a bridgehead from which he could swing to the Baltic and then south to meet the Russians.

Gavin protested that he had only one battalion at his disposal; the main body of his division was still on its way from Cologne by truck and train. Dempsey emphasised the political necessity behind the dash to the Baltic. Using Montgomery's arguments, he explained to Gavin that the Russians had to be headed off before they got to Denmark. Ridgway, who had worked with Gavin since North Africa, offered additional troops from General Stroh's 8th Infantry which was already on the Elbe. He insisted, however, that as he didn't know the 'Golden Arrow' division, as the 8th was called, too well, he, Gavin, should take charge of the Elbe operation. Dempsey concurred.

In the end Gavin gave in and agreed to attack the Elbe at about 4 am on the morning of the 30th. He did not realize that the crossing would result in the greatest triumph ever achieved by a single US division; soon a whole German army would surrender to the 10,000-odd paratroopers of the red, white and blue of the 'All American Division'.[6]

Thus while Gavin hastily planned his crossing, which might ensure Monty reached the Baltic before the Russians did, the British, dug in on the other side of their bridgehead, experienced their last counter-attack of the war.

The Cameronians were dug in with their right to the Elbe–Trave Canal and their left astride the main Dalldorf–Lauenburg road. During the night they consolidated their positions through which the Seaforths would attack the next day to capture Dalldorf the following day. Twice the Cameronians' CO sent out patrols to reconnoitre the road to the village and both times they reported no sign of the enemy.

At dawn an officer patrol crept down the road and almost at once bumped into the enemy advancing cautiously on the Cameronians' positions. They slipped away and were just making their report to Colonel Remington Hobbs, the Cameronians' CO, when the van of the German attack hit D Company. The young Germans belonged to a hastily-thrown-together understrength Division, but they attacked the Jocks with des-

6. So called on account of their tri-coloured shoulder patch.

74

perate energy. Even the terrific blast of small-arms fire and the artillery barrage the Cameronians called down were unable to stop them. They dug in right under the British positions and began to slog it out, forcing the Cameronians to retreat here and there in the face of their suicidal daring.

Now it was midday and the Cameronians' Brigade Commander, Brigadier Villiers, knew that the situation was serious. Prisoners had revealed that this was a determined full-scale attack. In addition he knew that as long as the youthful fanatics, who were fully prepared to die for their Führer at this late stage of the game, held the little wood they had seized from the Cameronians, the break-out to the north would be held up. He ordered the Seaforths to clear the wood—and clear it quick!

The Seaforths advanced across the field under thin rain. It had grown strangely quiet. They were about 100 yards from the dark fir wood. Still no sign of the enemy. Fifty yards. A young subaltern raised his hand. It was as if the movement signified something to the waiting men, hidden in the trees. There was a single pistol shot. In an instant the whole edge of the wood crackled with small-arms fire.

The Seaforths were galvanized into action. An officer waved his arm. A sergeant bellowed an order and with a roar, they began to run for the trees.

It took four hours. When it was over only four Germans remained alive. The Seaforths leaned exhausted on their weapons. The barrels of their brens gleamed with heat and piles of cartridge cases lay at their feet. They had won. The way ahead was clear. Behind them on the Basedow road they could already hear the rumble of the first tanks heading north. The race to the Baltic was on.

Twenty miles away on that same day the man who once had written, 'As a young man of pure British descent, some of whose forefathers have held high positions in the British Army, I have always been desirous of devoting what little capability and energy I may possess to the country which I love so dearly,' staggered into the underground studios of Hamburg Radio.

The little man, with his nose jammed on his face at an odd angle and a deep-set scar which ran from right ear to mouth, might have been exhausted or drunk. The two German technicians did not know and did not care. The man was a renegade—a traitor—and he was in for trouble now that the British were coming. Soon he would be arrested and all who had associated with him. Now he was come to make his last

75

broadcast before running for his life. Perhaps he needed the drink.

He was an Englishman, a traitor whose voice had been the best known (after Churchill's) and the best hated in the country from which he came, as he nightly poured out his snarling venom against the land that had nurtured him and that, in his heart, he had loved so much.

So William Joyce, alias 'Lord Haw-Haw', began to record his last broadcast, well aware that soon his life would come to a close at the end of a length of English rope. He spoke his piece with slow obstinate dignity. He ended with six carefully phrased sentences in that nasal voice of his which had sent shivers of rage and fear down the spines of his English listeners for so many years: 'Britain's victories are barren; they leave her poor and they leave her people hungry; they leave her bereft of markets and the wealth she possessed six years ago. But above all they leave her with an immensely greater problem than she had then.

'We are nearing the end of one phase in Europe's history, but the next will be no happier. It will be grimmer, harder and perhaps bloodier. And now I ask you earnestly can Britain survive? I am profoundly convinced that without German help she cannot...'

The mike went dead. The light changed from red to white. The engineer waved his hand. He rose to his feet to signify that the tape was finished.

Slowly the little man, who was to prove a better prophet than many a British cabinet minister at that moment of victory for the Empire, rubbed his eyes wearily; then he staggered out the way he had come. The hunt was on.

# II

# DECISION FOR DONITZ

'Es geht alles vorueber
Es geht alles vorbei
Nach jedem Dezember
Gibts wieder ein Mai.'
*Popular German song of the spring of 1945*

'It will all pass
It will all be over
After every December
There is always a May.'

# I

# The Race for the Baltic

## 30 APRIL–I MAY

'This is a proper Fred Karno's—this is!'
*British Paratrooper*

I

At almost exactly the same time as the Seaforths made their last attack on the River Elbe, three men in far away Berlin were standing, staring down at the face of their dead master, the man they had served for the last twelve years. It was covered with blood. In his lifeless fingers he still gripped the Walther PPK pistol. The man who had terrorized Europe for six years, whose name was hated from one end of the world to the other, had committed suicide. Adolf Hitler, Führer of the German People, was dead.

In silence, Martin Bormann, Hitler's fat undersized confidant of the last four years, stared down at the mutilated face of his master, behind whose back he had climbed to unprecedented power. Then he threw a glance at the Leader's longtime mistress and new wife. She lay on the couch, her shoes placed neatly on the carpet, her blue dress with its white cuffs carefully smoothed down over her knees—Hitler had been a bourgeois prude right to the end—her long blonde hair hanging loose. A strong acrid odour of cyanide came from her direction—so strong that those of the men present who were going to survive could detect its smell on their uniforms for days afterwards. Eva Braun was dead too.

Grunting, Bormann bent down and picked up Eva. The sight of her in Bormann's arms angered SS Sturmbannfuhrer Otto Günsche; he knew that Hitler's mistress had always hated the fat, toadlike Bormann. It angered the other man, SS Obersturmbannfuhrer Erich Kempka, too. He called to Günsche, 'I'll carry Eva,' and took her out of Bormann's arms, before the all-powerful Party Leader could protest. Bormann shrugged and let them get on with it.

79

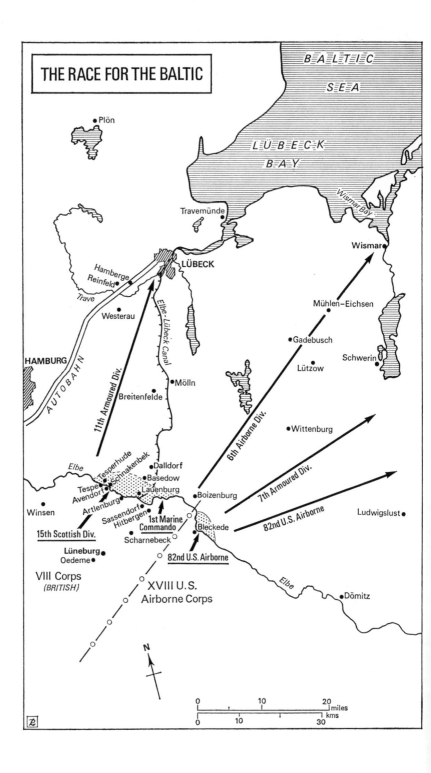

## THE RACE FOR THE BALTIC

BALTIC SEA

LÜBECK BAY

Wismar Bay

• Plön

Travemünde

Wismar•

**LÜBECK**

Hamberge
Reinfeld•

Mühlen–Eichsen
•

Trave

Westerau•

•Gadebusch

Schwerin•

Elbe–Lübeck Canal

Lützow•

HAMBURG

AUTOBAHN

11th Armoured Div.

•Mölln

Breitenfelde•

6th Airborne Div.

•Wittenburg

Elbe

•Dalldorf

Tesperhude
Schnakenbek
•Basedow

7th Armoured Div.

Winsen•

Tespe•
Avendorf•
Artlenburg•

Lauenburg•

•Boizenburg

Ludwigslust•

Artlenburg•
Sassendorf•
Hitbergen•
**1st Marine Commando**

•Bleckede

82nd U.S. Airborne

**15th Scottish Div.**

Scharnebeck ○

**Lüneburg**•
Oedeme•

○ **82nd U.S. Airborne**

Elbe

**VIII Corps**
*(BRITISH)*

○

**XVIII U.S. Airborne Corps**

•Dömitz

○

N

0        10        20 miles

0      10      30 kms

One wonders what went through Martin Bormann's head that afternoon in ruined Berlin with the sound of the Russian tank guns getting ever closer and closer. The *Reichsleiter*, who sent his wife in Bavaria full details of his sexual adventures with an actress,[1] was undoubtedly an opportunist. Over the last year or so he had wormed himself more and more into Hitler's favour so that in the end Hitler had found him indispensable. As a result Bormann, who was always there—day and night—when *mein Fuehrer* wanted him, had been able to cut out the influence of all the other major Nazi leaders—Goering, Himmler, Goebbels. Now Hitler was dead, the question posed itself: what was he to do? Was there still a chance for him to retain a position of power in Germany?

Goering and Himmler were now banned from the Party due to his actions. In his Will Hitler had written the day previously that they had 'brought irreparable shame on the country and the whole nation by secretly negotiating with the enemy without my knowledge and against my will'. As for Goebbels, the Minister of Propaganda intended to stay in Berlin and take the life of his wife, six children and of himself once the Russians penetrated the Hitler bunker. The way was free for a bold man to succeed to the empty throne, but who should that bold man be?

That afternoon Bormann must have considered all the possibilities until perhaps in the end, he decided he would contact Admiral Dönitz, Nazi commander in North-West Germany and since the day before, Hitler's official successor. The Admiral, who during most of the war had been in charge of the U-boats which had brought the British almost to their knees, was a fanatical Nazi but a man completely without political ability. For Bormann, 'the perfect prototype of a public servant without political opinions, bent on personal power and devoted to the service of authority'[2] who had taken five years of incessant work to build up his unique position, Dönitz would be an ideal instrument of his own personal ambitions. He began to draft a cable to the Admiral in far-off Plön in Schleswig-Holstein. It read:

Grand Admiral Dönitz.

In place of the former Reich-Marshal Goering, the Führer had designated you as his successor. Written authoriza-

1. His wife suggested that perhaps the three of them and their children could live together.
2. Edward Crankshaw: *Gestapo: Instrument of Tyranny* (New York: Putnam).

tion on the way. Immediately take all measures required by the present situation.

As he handed it to his secretary, Fraulein Else Krueger, he was pleased with himself. For the present Dönitz did not need to know that Hitler was dead; Hitler alive made him, Bormann, a more effective figure in the Admiral's eyes. With Hitler dead, he was nobody. Now he would make his plans for an escape out of the dying city. He would try to get to Dönitz in Plön and be the first bearer of the news of Hitler's death. In this way he could reduce to a minimum the period of his temporary eclipse and speedily revive his authority by his personal presence at Dönitz's HQ.

Bormann, the professional survivor, started to look around for companions for the hazardous journey.[3]

II

While Bormann planned his escape, Ridgway's XVIII Corps began to fight its way out of its bridgeheads on the Elbe. Gavin's crossing at Bleckede had gone well. The Elbe there was much narrower than at Artlenburg and the opposition had been minimal. The problem had been the German artillery which Ridgway felt was worse than that which had faced his Corps at the Rhine crossing and the automatic mines which the Germans had floated down the river among his assault boats. Now, however, all opposition had been overcome and with only light casualties Gavin's airborne troopers and the infantry of the 8th Division were fanning out over the flat countryside on the other side of the river. Once they had established themselves, he would turn General Hasbrouck's 7th Armoured Division loose to link up with the Russians.

But there was a problem. Dempsey wanted the prestige of the link-up to be gained by the British. The day before he had called the paratroop commander to his HQ and asked him if he couldn't let the 6th British Airborne have priority at the bridgeheads. It would mean a lot to the 'Red Devils' and the

3. As far as is known he never made it, but the world press have never been prepared to let him rest in peace. In August, 1971, a popular French paper headlines the news that 'Martin Bormann (is) behind the Kennedy Murders', and goes on to record an international band of killers located in Texas carried out the two assassinations at the German's command.

82

British Army. Ridgway didn't like the idea. He explained to Dempsey that 'this request would throw my attack off stride'. In addition to shooting Hasbrouck's 7th forward, he wanted the 82nd to push on. 'To permit the 6th Airborne to make the first contact meant that I would have to cut them diagonally across the zone of attack of the 7th Armoured, which would cause all sorts of trouble on the roads.'

Dempsey listened politely, but impatiently, as if people never spoke quickly enough for his fertile brain. Then he said, 'That's quite all right. I understand. You do it your own way.'

But back at his CP, Ridgway began to mull over Dempsey's request once again. He 'remembered the great fight the British had made throughout the war, the disaster of Dunkirk, the quiet valour of the people of England under the German bombings'. In the end he decided to grant Dempsey's request. He picked up the phone. He was going to 'turn Bols's[4] 6th British Airborne loose'.

Ridgway's emotions were undoubtedly genuine, but they smacked of the condescension of a representative of a great power to a second-class one living off old traditions and past victories; they revealed, too, how much the American attitude to the British had changed in these last months. But at Bols's HQ the staff officers of the 6th Airborne had no time to think about the reasons for the sudden go-ahead. Their problem was to get the 'Red Devils' organized and over the nearest bridge.

Today no one can satisfactorily explain how the red-bereted paratroopers, who had dropped on the Rhine a month before and in some battalions had suffered up to 40 per cent casualties, had been able to reorganize and without heavy weapons or transport to speak of had managed to fight their way to the Elbe. But Bols's men had done exactly that. At the beginning of their break-out from the Rhine bridgehead they had nothing but jeeps. Not for long, though. They seized anything with four wheels and an engine: post office trucks, butchers' vans, wood-burning truckers complete with stove-bearing trailer. Alan Moorhead, the war reporter, even noted one trooper 'dashing' forward at a steady 5 miles an hour in a looted steamroller!

Now they were on the Elbe and faced the worst problem of all. Although Ridgway wanted to turn them loose, they had no priority to cross Colonel Foster's heavily attacked bridges. The bridges at Artlenburg and Lauenburg were reserved for the 11th Armoured Division. What were they to do? While Gen-

4. Commander of the 6th Airborne.

eral Bols fumed at the delay, the staff officers sought in vain for an answer.

The 'Red Devils' soon solved their own problem. They were scheduled to cross with the lower priorities on the tanks of the Scots Greys, who had been assigned to assist them in their fight to the Baltic. Now they took the law into their own hands. Draping camouflage nets over the divisional signs of the Scots Greys' tanks and turning their red berets inside out so that the black inner lining made them look like armoured troops, they approached the bridge boldly. Their plan was to make it appear that they were just another unit of the 11th Armoured. As they approached the bridge—for once not under attack by German jets—they saw the MPs eyeing them curiously. They knew the 'Redcaps' had orders to turn everything back save the high-priority 11th Armoured traffic. Now rumbling up the slope to the bridge some of them felt a flutter in their stomachs. One false move and they'd be off the road waiting impotently for another chance to cross the river. The first tank began to clatter up the metal ramp. The MP directing the traffic looked at them hard. His critical eyes swept across the handful of paratroopers crouched on the tank's deck. Then he waved his arm. They could move on. They had pulled it off! Triumphantly the first tank started to rumble across the bridge. Behind it another followed and another. The 'Red Devils' were across and on their way to the Baltic.

III

Grand Admiral Karl Dönitz received Bormann's message at six-fifteen. It came as a complete surprise to him. He had known Bormann since 1943, but the fat little man had not registered in his mind. For him the Führer's secretary had been a 'nobody, neither up nor down'. Why had Bormann picked him?

He was gradually becoming aware of the full impact of the message which his adjutant had just brought him. It meant, in essence, that he was in control and could at least make decisions. The slip of coarse paper which lay on the desk in front of him meant that his impotence of these last weeks had vanished.

For days now Dönitz had been considering suicide. The man who was generally regarded in the Allied camp as the hard-hearted, cold-blooded originator of 'unrestricted submarine warfare' had had enough. Daily his staff brought him terrible reports of the suffering of the hundreds of thousands of German refugees from the East struggling by land and sea to the 'safety' of the West. They were undergoing indescribable miseries: rape and murder at the hands of the Russians; bombing and machine-gunning from the planes of the Western Allies. And his Navy, the pride of his life, could do nothing at all to alleviate the suffering of these people. As a result he had been considering making his separate peace with the West, surrendering what was left of the *Kriegsmarine* to them and then taking his own life; he would never tolerate the indignity of spending a second term of imprisonment in a British POW camp as he had done in the last year of World War I.

Now all had changed. He could do something! The medium-sized Admiral with the piercing gaze and cold pale face started to make plans.

Karl Dönitz had been born in 1891 in Berlin, the descendant of a long line of Prussian officers and Lutheran pastors, though his long upturned nose and high cheekbones revealed Slavic blood. As a child he had been brought up in the strict, dour Prussian traditions of self-sacrifice and submission to the state and authority—his father had once remarked he would allow himself 'to be chopped to pieces' for *his* Kaiser. In 1910 young Karl had entered the Navy and had served on cruisers till 1915 when he had transferred to the newest arm of the Imperial Service—the primitive U-boat. Two years later he was in command of a submarine attacking a heavily laden convoy off Sicily, when a British destroyer had taken a direct course on his boat. It all happened so suddenly that Dönitz barely had time to yell '*crash dive!*' Desperately the crew fumbled with the controls. Just before the British boat rammed them, they submerged. But the rapid dive had affected the boat's steering. At dawn on the following day *U-68* suddenly popped to the surface—right in the middle of the convoy! Everywhere the alarmed Allied destroyers started pumping 5-inch shells in Dönitz's direction. Hastily the young lieutenant ordered his crew to abandon ship. Moments later he joined them to be fished ignominiously out of the water at the end of a boat-hook by grinning British tars.

It was then that Dönitz experienced his first taste of POW camps. One day he would do over ten years in them. But that was much later. Now the young sailor tried to escape or to get an early discharge on medical grounds. Together with two comrades he pretended to go mad, running around his quarters miming a submarine in action. The British doctors were not impressed. The sudden 'mental breakdown' was speedily cured by a spell of solitary confinement. But in the end Dönitz succeeded in his plan. By swallowing large quantities of tobacco, he produced the symptoms of blackwater fever and was discharged.

In July 1919, he rejoined the German Navy and because submarines were banned under the terms of the *Versaillesdiktat* he went into destroyers, steadily working himself up the ladder of rank through hard work and inflexible devotion to his service. From 1930 to 1934 he was the staff officer responsible for preparing measures to meet what were called 'internal disturbances' and it was in the depressed early thirties that he first started to find himself attracted to the Nazi Party. For him it offered, in this period of chaos and uncertainty, discipline and hope. Besides, Hitler had promised a strong German military force if he ever came to power.

When, in 1933, Hitler achieved this aim, Dönitz, unlike many of the older Navy officers, supported him. Thereafter promotion was rapid and as Dönitz admitted after the war at his Nuremberg Trial: 'Naturally I admired and joyfully recognized the high authority of Adolf Hitler because he succeeded in realizing his national and social aims without spilling blood.'

When Hitler began to 'spill blood' in 1939, Dönitz still supported him. As the war progressed Hitler started to lose faith in the Navy's big ships and the admirals whose pride they were. He turned more and more to the U-boats and the man who controlled them—Karl Dönitz. Thus when the traditionalist head of the German *Kriegsmarine*, Admiral Raeder, resigned in 1943, Hitler appointed Dönitz in his place.

Now the Admiral grew very close to his Führer. He spent long periods at Hitler's headquarters and as the latter knew very little of naval affairs, he enjoyed more freedom of speech and action than did the generals such as Keitel and Jodl. Even when the British anti-submarine tactics triumphed over Dönitz's most feared weapon, the electrically powered submarine, Hitler did not lose confidence in his Grand Admiral. In March he appointed him virtual dictator of the natural fuel resources of the Reich and head of the Merchant Marine. He also told him that if for some reason Germany was split up by the Allied advances, he, Dönitz, would be in charge of the North-Western German defences. Now he was in almost constant daily attendance at Hitler's Headquarters.

In spite of the ruins around him Dönitz did not lose faith in Adolf Hitler. When it was clear to even the most stupid man-

86

in-the street that Germany's war was lost, Dönitz could declare on 11 April, 1945, with the Americans already on the Elbe, that, 'At the latest in one year—perhaps even in this year— Europe will realise that Adolf Hitler is the only statesman of any stature in Europe!'

This, then, was the man who was soon to rule what was left of Hitler's Third Reich—a man who preferred to ignore the smouldering ruins all about him, who avoided controversy and counter-argument by seeing as few politicians as possible and surrounding himself with trusted naval officers, and who as late as 21 April when he saw Hitler for the last time, was prepared to fight to the last man for the defence of North Germany.

Dönitz's first action was in keeping with his past and con-firmed the worst fears of those close to him who wanted the war brought speedily to an end. He drafted a telegram to the already dead Adolf Hitler, which read:

My Führer!
My loyalty to you will be unconditional. I shall do every-thing possible to relieve you in Berlin. If Fate nevertheless compels me to rule the Reich as your appointed successor, I shall continue this war to an end worthy of the unique, heroic struggle of the German people.
Grand Admiral Dönitz

It was now nearly midnight, and Dönitz knew he would have to move swiftly if he were to secure the amazing new power that had descended upon him so surprisingly. At Plön his headquarters was dominated by the hard-faced troops of SS Leader Himmler's bodyguard, his only rival for leadership. Two days before he had offered his support to Himmler. Now everything had changed and he realized that the time had come to eradicate his rival. He summoned his adjutant Com-mander Lüdde-Neurath to his office and told him, 'Telephone Himmler and tell him I want to see him in Plön.'

The young sailor hesitated. 'But what if he causes trouble. sir?' he asked. 'Don't you think we should have Cremer's men here just in case? You need protection, sir.'

Dönitz pondered the remark. Lt-Commander Cremer was a former U-boat commander who had formed an anti-tank bat-talion out of submariners without boats. Ten days before, his battalion had launched a daring commando raid into British-held territory near Hamburg and had destroyed twenty tanks of the British 7th Armoured Division—the famous 'Desert

Rats'. If there was to be trouble, Cremer was the man to handle it. 'All right,' he said. 'Get Cremer's men. But see that he places them round the building in a way that Himmler won't notice them.'

It was exactly midnight when Heinrich Himmler arrived. His reply to Neurath's call had been a blunt 'no' and Dönitz himself had been forced to call him before he had agreed to come. Now he was there, protected by six hulking SS giants, armed with machine-pistols, who looked eager for trouble. Dönitz shot a glance at his adjutant.

The young sailor reacted at once. 'Would the gentlemen care for a drink?' he asked with a smile, heading them off before they could follow their boss into Dönitz's office. Taking the first one by the arm, he led them away to the officers' mess.

Himmler sat down, still clad in his ankle-length greatcoat.

Nervously the Admiral cleared his throat and stretched out his hand to the pile of papers on the desk for reassurance. Beneath them he had taken the precaution of hiding a small Browning pistol. If it came to a showdown with Himmler, he was ready to shoot first. 'I would like you to read this?' he said, passing the telegram over to Himmler. 'It appoints me as the Führer's successor.'

The SS Chief snatched the paper. An expression of astonishment spread over his sallow face. Then he went pale. All hope collapsed visibly. For a second he sat there lifeless, the telegram dangling from his thin fingers; then he staggered to his feet and bowed. 'Allow me, Admiral,' he said weakly, 'to be the second man in your state.'

Dönitz, feeling stronger at the other man's meek surrender to his new authority, shook his head. 'No, Himmler, I can't allow that.'

Their conversation continued into the small hours, but when Himmler left he knew he was finished. Apart from the police who were still loyal to him, he no longer had the power to force Dönitz's hand. He was finished and from now until the day on which he finally slipped from Dönitz's HQ for good, the most feared man in Europe was reduced to hanging around the corridors of power—or what was left of them—unnoticed by anyone, even the most junior officers.

As he lay in bed unable to sleep in the early hours of that morning, the Admiral considered his situation. Goering, Hitler's long-time successor until the Führer had become aware of his treachery, was under arrest somewhere in Bavaria.[5] Goebbels and Bormann were still in Berlin. Himmler had now been removed from his power. As for Ribbentrop, Speer, Keitel, Jodl, they were *'kleine Fische'* (little fish); they didn't count. Now he was the only one left with power at his disposal, based on the arms of the 2,000,000-odd soldiers still under his command in North-West Germany, Denmark and Holland. But as he finally dropped into an uneasy sleep in the first hours of 1 May, 1945—the traditional German day of celebration and hope-Dönitz had still not decided whether he would fight or not. One thing, however, was clear. Everything depended upon how long Field-Marshal Busch's men could hold the line of the Elbe against Montgomery's advancing men. Once the latter reached the Baltic and sealed off the German escape route to the West from Mecklenburg, everything would be lost; there would be no more use fighting.

### IV

At eleven o'clock on the morning of 1 May Martin Bormann dispatched another message to Admiral Dönitz. It was as enigmatic as the first. It read:

> The testament is in force. Coming to you as soon as possible. Till then you should in my opinion refrain from public statement.
>
> Bormann.

This naturally increased Dönitz's suspicions that the Führer was dead and that for some reason Bormann was concealing the fact. In reality Bormann was waiting for news from General Krebs whom he had sent to the Russians to try to arrange some sort of truce for the inhabitants of the *Führerbunker*. Until he knew what the Russians intended to do with them, Dönitz would have to be content with the strange message.

Dönitz knew that he should tell his people that Hitler was dead, but he was scared of the chaos that might result. As a result, he decided to go along with Bormann and make only the most pressing decisions until he knew for certain that Hitler was dead. He radioed the German commanders in the occupied countries still under Nazi control in an attempt to

5. He wasn't. Goering's own *Luftwaffe* troops had freed him from SS imprisonment.

avoid any unnecessary bloodshed with the local resistance movements. In particular, he told General Lindemann in Denmark, who was a fervent Nazi, to restrain his men. Then he called Ribbentrop, the Nazi Foreign Minister, and asked him whom he would recommend as his successor. An hour passed before Ribbentrop called him back. 'I've thought about this problem over and and over, and I can propose one man only capable of doing the job—*myself.*'

Dönitz felt 'like laughing in his face'. But politely he turned down Ribbentrop's offer. Instead he asked former Rhodes Scholar and Nazi Finance Minister Schwerin von Krosigk to take over the post. The Finance Minister, whom the Nazis had contemptuously called the 'paymaster' and had only noticed when they needed the funds, accepted the post gladly, although Dönitz told him: 'You can expect to win no laurels, but you and I are bound by duty to accept our tasks in the interests of the German people.'

A little while later Himmler heard of the new appointment. He called von Krosigk to his quarters. 'I hear you're going to be the new Foreign Minister,' he said slowly. 'I can only congratulate you. Never has a Foreign Minister had greater opportunities. In a few days the Russians and Americans will clash and then we, the Germans, will be the decisive force. Never has the aim of getting to the Ural Mountains been closer to fulfilment than at this moment.'

Von Krosigk pulled himself together. 'Do you still think you personally have a task to fulfil?' he asked sarcastically.

Himmler was a man completely without humour. One of his intimates had once said of him that 'he had his feet planted squarely—two feet above the ground!' He did not notice the sarcasm. 'Oh yes,' he answered eagerly. 'I am a rock of order. And Eisenhower and Montgomery are going to recognize me as such. All I need is an hour's talk with either of them, and the matter will be settled.' That morning Dönitz held his first conference with his chief military advisers—Field-Marshal Keitel and Colonel-General Jodl. The two men, for whom the hangman's noose was already waiting in the Allied camp, went along with Dönitz's ideas on what to do next. Elderly Field-Marshal Busch, whose men were doing the fighting on the Elbe, did not. Busch was all for offensive action against the British in the Hamburg area; and he knew that he had the support of General Lindemann in Denmark, a convinced Nazi, who had considerable troop reserves in that country. Dönitz turned down Busch's suggestion. As he saw it, General Wolz, the Commandant of the besieged city, would have to remain on the defensive; why anger the British unnecessarily? Busch turned on the sailor angrily, and made what Minister of War Production Albert Speer, who was present, called later, 'a great to do about the Grand Admiral no longer acting in Hitler's spirit'.

But Dönitz was no longer interested in such idealistic notions. He ended the Field-Marshal's tirade swiftly and explained his major concern was keeping the Lübeck–Elbe gap open so that the hundreds of thousands of civilians and soldiers fleeing westwards from the Russians could reach the safety of the West. In other words, all he expected of Busch was that he stopped Montgomery's drive to the Baltic.

With that the conference ended and Dönitz went to his office to reply to a telegram he had received earlier from Erich Kaufmann, the Gauleiter of besieged Hamburg. Kaufmann, who in the last two years had gone sour on the whole Nazi creed after Hitler had refused to visit the city to console the survivors of the terrible July, 1943, raids in which eight days of RAF bombing had resulted in 30,000 dead and three-quarters of the city being destroyed, had wired: 'The Wehrmacht is fighting in this area according to the principle that every town and every village must be defended. This means the senseless and complete destruction of towns and villages ... and that the Western enemy is temporarily held up while the Bolsheviks push on into Mecklenburg without hindrance.'

Dönitz replied, 'Everything possible is being done to stop the Russian advance into Mecklenburg ... and allow the withdrawal of the German population. But this withdrawal is only possible if a door to the East is kept open. If the Elbe–Trave Canal is blocked by the British we will be sacrificing seven million valuable Germans to the caprice of the Russians ... we must defend the Elbe positions with the utmost determination!'

Hardly had Dönitz dispatched the message to Kaufmann, when a chance encounter with Himmler who was still hanging around the HQ after the previous evening's showdown, told him that it all had been in vain. He and Speer were going for a hasty lunch when they bumped into the SS Leader. Although he had no special liking for the ex-chicken farmer, who lived in a strange exotic world of his own, complete with astrologers and weird anthropologists, Dönitz did not feel he could treat a man who, until a few days ago, had held so much power with contempt. So he invited him to lunch with Speer and himself.

Over the meagre meal, Himmler dropped a bomb. Through his own sources he had discovered that Gauleiter Kaufmann intended to surrender the city of Hamburg without a fight. In fact he had already started discussing the surrender with the representatives of the British 7th Armoured Division and was having a leaflet printed on the proposed surrender for the city's population.

Dönitz's normally pale face flushed an angry red. 'If everybody acts on his own,' he exploded, 'my assignment no longer has any point.'

Speer tried to appease him. He offered to drive to Hamburg in spite of the fact that Allied planes dominated the roads and were shooting up anything that moved during the daylight hours. Dönitz gave his approval and a little later Speer set off, fighting his way through the jumble of military vehicles, civilian cars, and horse-drawn carts steadily streaming northwards away from the advancing British.

Meanwhile Dönitz called in his long-time associate Admiral von Friedeburg, a skilled negotiator and the new head of what was left of the German Navy. Swiftly he told him what he wanted him to do. 'As soon as the British force their way to the Baltic and we don't have the open door any more [i.e. the escape route westwards], I'm going to send you to Montgomery. Keep close to the telephone now at all times.'

Speer, the brilliant architect who had been perhaps Hitler's only friend but who a few days before had been prepared to murder his benefactor by forcing poison gas down the airshaft of the Berlin *Führerbunker*, found Kaufmann had made up his mind to surrender. Well protected from Dönitz's rage and the attempts of the *Werwolf* organization[6] to murder him, Speer found him surrounded by his heavily armed bodyguard of students from Hamburg University.

Kaufmann did not pull his punches. He showed Speer the ultimatum the 7th Armoured had sent to General Wolz, the battle commandant of the city. It read:

Before attacking Bremen we demanded the surrender of the City. As this offer was refused, we had no alternative but to attack with artillery and air support. Bremen fell in 24 hours but not without much unnecessary bloodshed ... The population of Hamburg will not easily forget its first large-scale raid by over one thousand heavy bombers. We now dispose of a bomber force five to ten times greater numerically and operating from nearby airfields. After the war, the

6. The Nazi resistance organization. For further details, see *Werewolf* by the same author, published by Leo Cooper Ltd.

German people must be fed: the more Hamburg's dock installations are damaged, the greater are the chances of famine in Germany.

If this offer is refused, we shall have no alternative but to attack Hamburg with all the forces at our disposal.

He pointed to the last sentence and said to Speer: 'Am I supposed to follow the example of the Gauleiter of Bremen? He issued a proclamation calling on the people to defend themselves to the last and then cleared out while the city was demolished by an air raid.'

Kaufmann added that there was already a threat of open rebellion in the notoriously 'red' city. After all even Hitler rarely dared to visit the port with its long-time communist tradition. For his part, he was so determined not to allow 'his' city to suffer any more that he would mobilize the masses to active resistance to the Army if the latter attempted to continue the battle.

Speer knew when he was beaten; besides, Kaufmann was acting as he would have done himself if he had been charged with the control of the city. Something, he knew, must be saved from the wreck of the Third Reich so that life could go on after the battle was over. He reached for the telephone.

Dönitz was angry at Kaufmann's decision. He tried to argue, but Speer told him of the threat of open rebellion. The Admiral gave in and asked for one hour to consider the situation. Before the hour was up, he called Speer again and told him to direct Kaufmann to surrender the city to the British. The vital Elbe defence line upon which his whole policy depended was crumbling fast.

v

The order of march of the Red Devils on that sunny May Day was simple but suicidal. One section of the Recce group advanced on a centre line, with a section of infantry on the minor roads to right and left of the major one. Behind these three sections came the bulk of the parachute brigade riding on the tanks of the Scots Greys. It was a tricky tactic—a thin arrow of under-armed infantry pushing forward into German territory packed full of German troops, who could cut them off at will.

But in the heady atmosphere of that last great drive, the

93

paras were prepared to take risks; a spirit of desperate heroism —almost fatalism—seemed to possess these soldiers who had fought so hard in Normandy, the Ardennes and on the Rhine. At Lützow they found the cobbled main street packed as far as the eye could see with a chaotic mess of German civilians and fleeing infantry. Sergeant Stewart of the leading tank bellowed to the paras on the deck to watch out and then opened fire. The Besa sent a stream of bullets over the heads of the crowd. Panic-stricken they fled in all directions or dropped to the cobbles, heads clasped in arms. The advance roared on.

They clattered through Gadebusch. It was packed full of Germans. The Red Devils simply ignored them. The Germans did the same. German military policemen, their metal plates of authority around their necks (the silver plates gave them the nicknames of 'chain-dogs' among the German soldiery), waved them on, not knowing what else to do. Now the fields on either side were filled with Panthers and foxholes full of German infantry. But none fired. So the Red Devils drove on.

Mühlen Eichsen! They had no maps left now and were using the yellow and black German road signs to guide them. The air was getting cooler. There was the smell of the sea in the breeze from the north. Twenty kilometres to Wismar and the Baltic Sea!

Sergeant Randall in one of the lead tanks radioed back that he was held up by a German troop train, armed with three self-propelled guns. It was steaming slowly across a level crossing, What was he to do? His squadron leader's voice crackled over the air. 'Let it go by! Not worth blocking the road by knocking it out.'

So Sergeant Randall sat calmly on his turret and waited till the train had passed. Then he tapped his driver's shoulder and they were on their way again.

It was now mid-morning. Suddenly a flight of fighters swept down low over the column. The Red Devils tensed. They were sitting ducks and there was no room to turn and no cover to be found in the bare fields on both sides of the narrow high crowned road. The Messerschmitts zoomed down the whole length of the column at treetop height. The noise was deafening and the paras ducked instinctively. But there was no chatter of machine-guns or roar of rockets. The Germans were just checking them out. If they had been Russian, they would have reacted differently, the relieved paratroopers learned later. The advance continued. The paratroopers were within striking distance of their objective.

The Germans were in full retreat. Cars, heavily laden with officers and their baggage, honked their way through the traffic jams—the piled up confusion of the civilian treks[7] and military convoys. Guns slithered into ditches and were abandoned. A truck here and there ran out of petrol. Then the driver would thrust a couple of stick grenades, tied crudely together, into its engine. A crump, a spurt of violet flame, and that would be that. They'd begin to walk. Tanks, self-propelled guns, dental trucks, mobile workshops, 10-ton Mercedes—they were all being abandoned now. The Army walked or jogged along on straw-filled carts, pulled by lean flea-bitten horses stolen from the protesting local farmers. The British were coming!

On that May Day when by tradition, German men, dressed in their best clothes celebrated liberally in the country pubs, garlanding themselves and their vehicles with the 'May Green' —branches of the newly green trees—the British fighters had a field day. They hedge-hopped across the flat Schleswig-Holstein countryside, machine-guns chattering, leaving behind them a shambles of molten metal and bloody broken bodies.

While the RAF blasted a path for the paratroopers, the 11th Armoured Division was also fighting its way forward towards its objective—the Hansa city of Lübeck on the Baltic. But it was finding the going tough. By midday its advance was starting to slow down. The narrow country roads were badly cratered and in places, impassable. Desperately the squadron leaders tried to find alternative routes, twisting and turning down cobbled, high-crowned village roads with their treacherous wide sandy verges.

The 23rd Hussars, for instance, stopped by bad cratering just short of Breitenfelde swung on to a small side road which simply gave way under the weight of their vehicles. Now the 2nd Fife and Forfar Yeomanry, carrying the infantry of the 1st Cheshires, was in the lead. Half a mile south of Reinfeld they had a stroke of luck. They swung on to the great German autobahn. The road to Lübeck was open.

To their rear the 23rd Hussars finally extricated themselves from the mess. Hurriedly loading the 8th Rifle Brigade on their tanks, they clattered after their rivals. Two hours later they caught up. Now both groups were directed on Lübeck, The 23rd was to follow the autobahn the whole way, while the Yeomanry was to branch off at Hamberge and take the good road from there to Lübeck.

7. German name given to officially organized civilian refugee columns.

95

The advance pressed on. By mid-afternoon the twin medieval spires of the Lübeck Gate were within sight. Here and there lone machine-gunners or desperate Hitler Youth snipers tried to hold up their advance. But they were almost there. Nothing was going to stop them now.

VI

At just after three that afternoon Admiral Dönitz received another message in code from Bormann in Berlin. Speer, who had just returned from Hamburg, was present when Lüdde-Neurath brought it in and observed closely as Dönitz's pale face began to flush. It read:

Grand Admiral Dönitz (Top Secret! Only via officer).

Führer deceased yesterday at 3.30 pm. Testament of 29 April appoints you Reich President, Minister Goebbels Chancellor, Reichsleiter Bormann Party Minister, Minister Seyss-Inquart Foreign Minister. On the Führer's instructions the testament sent out of Berlin to you and Field-Marshal Schorner,[8] to assure its preservation for the people.

Reichsleiter Bormann will try to get to you today, to orient you on the situation. The form and time of announcement to the troops and public are left to you.

Confirm receipt.

Goebbels  Bormann

Angrily he looked up at Speer and the young adjutant. 'This is utterly impossible!' he exploded, waving the piece of paper which had made him chief of the dying German state.

Speer realized what he meant. The message made a farce of his new office; Bormann and Goebbels were obviously going to make themselves the powers behind the throne.

Dönitz looked up at Lüdde-Neurath. 'Has anyone else seen the radio message yet?'

The young naval officer replied in the negative. Apart from himself and the radioman who had received it no one knew of its existence.

Dönitz ordered that the radioman should be sworn to secrecy, while the message itself should be locked away in the safe.

8. German Army commander in the South.

While Lüdde-Neurath went to carry out the order, Dönitz turned to Speer and asked: 'What will we do if Bormann and Goebbels actually arrive here?'

Then he continued resolutely: 'I absolutely will not co-operate with them in any case.'

Speer, who deeply hated Martin Bormann, concurred and the two men agreed to arrest both him and Goebbels if they turned up at the Plön HQ.[9]

The confirmation of his new office and the power to act that went with it finally rid Dönitz of his mood of depression which had hung over him these last weeks. An old friend, Admiral Godt, who visited him in his office a little while after he had received the Bormann message found him 'developing his views with Speer in a lively manner, full of initiative'. 'There's been enough fighting,' he told Godt. 'We must keep the state together. There must be no more unnecessary sacrifice of blood ...' The visitor thought the words 'fairly bubbled' out of the normally laconic Grand Admiral, but as he was to write later: 'My impression on that evening was of a complete change in Dönitz, now that he had been freed from the immediate influence of Hitler; it was almost as if he had been liberated from a nightmare. A few days before I would still have believed him capable of ordering total war without any regard to the consequences.'

As the afternoon of 1 May came to an end, Dönitz felt he had achieved some sort of order out of the chaos all around him. He had formed a government of sorts, with Count Schwerin von Krosigk and Albert Speer as its main members. He had cut himself off from all association with those prominent Nazis, whom he knew the Allies would soon be looking for, such as Himmler, Bormann and Goering. And he had reached an agreement with his generals that although they would not undertake any offensive action against Montgomery's British Army, they would still continue to fight the Russians and hold on to the vital Elbe line. As he prepared himself for bed the exhausted Admiral felt that he had shored up the wreck a little longer.

9. They needed not have feared. Goebbels committed suicide the following day and Bormann, with a couple of companions, disappeared completely to become post-war mystery number one. Since then he has been sought all over the world, variously disguised as a monk, a coffee farmer, the man behind the Kennedy murders, etc., etc. Recently ex-German Secret Service Chief General Gehlen makes the sensational disclosure that Bormann was a Soviet spy throughout the war and that he died in 1968 in the Soviet Union.

## VII

The first elements of the 6th Airborne—eleven light Honey
tanks and their load of Canadian paratroopers—reached the
edge of the Baltic seaport of Wismar at one o'clock that afternoon. For a while the men considered what to do next. It
seemed that it was up to them to capture the port. But how?
Before them lay two undamaged bridges leading into the
north-western part of Wismar. While they considered their
position, a German officer strolled up to them and suggested
calmly that he should take them across.

They hesitated. What if the bridges were mined or this was
some sort of trap? But in the end the officer's very calmness
convinced them. Perched on the leading tank, they began to
rumble across the bridges.

That had been at one o'clock. Now two hours later they
were spreading out into the north-western suburbs. One group
was approaching an airfield not marked on any maps available
to them when suddenly with a terrifying howl German jets
screamed down on them. The Red Devils ducked hastily. But
the planes zoomed over their heads without firing. The paratroopers breathed again and pressed on towards the strangely
silent *Luftwaffe* field. Suddenly a German sprang out of a ditch.
He flung a grenade at the commander of the leading tank. It
missed. The German did not get a second chance. The officer
raised his ·38 and fired. The German pitched forward, dead.

There was some further sporadic firing, then a bedraggled
German officer ran up, hands up above his head. 'I'm sorry we
fired on you,' he panted to the astonished troopers. 'But we
didn't realize you were British. Give us five minutes and we'll
surrender.' While he was trying to get his men to come out of
their hiding-places, a light plane tried to take off on the field.
A Honey sped after it. Plane and tank raced down the runway,
the latter pumping shell after shell at its target. But the German plane bore a charmed life. While the Honey raced to the
end of the tarmac and braked suddenly just before a ditch, the
plane rose into the air and escaped. Moments later the German officer re-emerged from the concrete bunker into which
he'd gone. Behind filed over two hundred dirty *Landser*,[10]
hands raised obediently above their heads in token of surrender. An astonished Red Devil, mouth open in amazed be-

10. German Army slang for the common soldier—equivalent to
'Tommy'.

wilderment, breathed; 'This is a proper Fred Karno's—this is!'[11]

But the 'battle' for Wismar was not all a 'proper Fred Karno's.' Major Watts, a doctor with the 6th Airborne, was to witness a tragedy on that day of victory for the paratroopers who had suffered such heavy losses during the war and seen six of their battalions completely wiped out. Just as his jeep convoy approached the outskirts, it bumped into a pitiful column of German Army wounded. Here and there the blood still seeped through the paper bandages of the seriously wounded as they dragged each other along. Exhausted Red Cross nurses in blood-stained aprons tried to help the amputees who hopped on with the rest of the column or lay immobile in little handcarts, screaming now and again when the wooden wheels bounced over a cobble. In all, the miserable frightened array stretched 2 miles along the road. Major Watts ordered his driver to halt. He approached the first nurse and asked her what was going on. She told him that they had been travelling in a troop train which had run out of fuel just outside Wismar. While they were wondering what to do next, a Cossack patrol had descended on them. They had sacked the train, robbing even the dying and shooting anyone who resisted. Before leaving they had swept the whole train with machine-gun fire.

Watts ordered his men to select the worst cases and put them on the stretchers attached to the medical jeeps. He told the nurses to stay where they were until he could bring help. Five minutes later he set off for a Luftwaffe hospital in the neighbourhood, returning to where the German column had been as soon as he had dumped his load. But the Germans had already gone. Their fear of the Russians was so intense that nothing could arrest their slow and painful progress to the West.

Late that afternoon, after an amazing 60 miles advance in eight hours, the leading brigade of the 6th Airborne started to drive through the streets of Wismar. Everywhere the windows and doors of the medieval houses were locked and barred. The whole town was dead. The inhabitants had barricaded themselves in, fearing that the Russians would arrive first. As the Red Devils clattered victoriously through the streets they could sense the Germans hidden behind the closed doors and windows, hearts thumping with fear at the rumble of the

11. World War I expression for what the Americans called a 'snafu'—a military mess—named after a popular comedian of the time.

Honeys, waiting for the knock on the door and the strange foreign voice, '*Frau—komm Frau—Davoi!* . . . *Frau, du schlafen!*'

But at that moment the paratroopers had time neither for the citizens' fears nor for their women. They were worried that they might be running into a trap. A sinister quiet hung over the town.

Captain Titch Wade MC, of the 3rd Para Engineer Squadron, followed by Sapper Jones, the only regular in the Squadron, burst into the little port office. Jones brandished his looted Schmeisser machine-pistol. The Germans' hands shot up. Titch ordered them to drop their weapons. The group of sailors, soldiers and civilians in uniform unbuckled their pistols. They pushed on.

An hour later when their patrols had penetrated to the city's limits they realized that Wismar was completely undefended. They had won the race to the Baltic!

It was at nine o'clock precisely that the first Russians of the 2nd Belorussian Army arrived from the East. With two motorcycle combinations in the lead, followed by two lease-lend American scout cars, containing seven ragged soldiers and one lone female armed with a tommy gun, they approached the paratroopers' positions cautiously. As they came closer, the paras could see their fingers crooked around the triggers of their weapons. Then they recognized the British uniform. They relaxed. Thereupon followed the handshaking, backslapping, the vodka and the dumbshow with the exaggerated gestures of goodwill and eternal friendship. Then abruptly the Russians turned, as if at some unspoken command. They got into their shabby vehicles and returned the way they had come. One hour later while the exhausted paras stretched out in their requisitioned beds, they began to build a monstrous roadblock on the outskirts of Wismar. The Iron Curtain was descending.[12]

12. It is interesting to note Bradley's comment on this operation. He would not even allow the British this minor triumph. After complaining that the 'British had been badgering Eisenhower for the attachment of an Amercan corps . . . for his push beyond the Elbe', he notes that this corps (Ridgway's) 'struck across the Elbe south of Hamburg towards the Baltic port of Lübeck to save Denmark for the West'.

# 2

# The Long Surrender

## 2–5 MAY, 1945

'Not so bad, a million chaps—good egg!'
*Field-Marshal Montgomery*

I

The big German staff officer sweated. As representative of
General Wolz, commander of Hamburg, he knew he was fighting for the life of Germany's greatest port and the last bastion
on Dönitz's Elbe Line. But the triumphant young British
officers of the 7th Armoured Division's staff were prepared to
make no concessions. As he sat in the airless little room in the
tiny hamlet of Meilsen, listening to the interpreter in his Oxford scarf, which he had insisted on wearing to impress the
British with his culture, he knew that General Wolz must surrender Hamburg. The port lay in ruins. It had died in the
four-day raid of 1943 and now, two years later, its centre was a
stony desert. Now too the city was crowded with the pathetic
refugees from the East who had fled from the Russians in long
covered wagon trains like the pioneers of the American West.
Could he allow these people to suffer the horror of an all-out
British attack on the city? Besides the city's hospitals were
filled to overflowing with the wounded who were still manag-
ing to get through from the East. They were quartered everywhere from primary schools to the great houses of the Hamburg *Prominenz*, where they lay, their blood-caked torn uniforms crawling with lice and their wounds alive with maggots,
while thirteen- and fourteen-year-old schoolgirls undressed
them ready for the surgeons.

The port's defenders were a collection of military flotsam—
the battered remnants of a proud Army. Marines, panzer
grenadiers, gunners, Luftwaffe men and infantry, all of them
dirty and dejected, collected at the point of a sub-machine-gun
by the 'chain dogs' and forced into the line. Except for a few
SS units and the officer cadet battalions, the German staff

officer knew that Wolz's command was worthless as a fighting formation. But the staff officers of the 'Desert Rat' division, which had fought the Germans all the way from Africa, showed no sympathy. They wanted Hamburg and Wolz was going to give it to them. While faraway in Plön, Admiral Dönitz slept exhausted after his first day as the new ruler of what was left of Germany, the staff officer finally gave in. He would return to Wolz and tell him that the British would accept nothing short of unconditional surrender.

The German got to his feet and while the British were blindfolding the interpreter with his own Christ Church scarf[1] asked if he could speak privately to the 7th Armoured Division Brigadier in charge of the British team. The Desert Rat nodded his agreement and the two men walked off together. When the German Colonel thought he was safe from being overheard, he said, 'General, this is purely personal. On behalf of General Wolz I want to ask your advice. Will we be sent to Siberia. Should I and the rest of the staff commit suicide, do you think?'

The Brigadier looked at him, shocked. 'That's entirely up to you.'

The discussion was over. Sadly the Colonel and his interpreter let themselves be led back to the German lines to break the news of the British stipulation to General Wolz, their minds full of what might befall them if the British handed them over to the Russians.

But where were the Russians? General Ridgway, commander of the XVIII Airborne Corps, needed to know that if his men were to avoid firing by accident on Rokossovsky's Belorussians. Since the 6th Airborne had met them the day before in Wismar, he knew it wouldn't be long before Gavin's 82nd Airborne bumped into them; and the paratroopers had itchy fingers. Shoot first and ask questions later—that was their motto.

That morning he ordered the only armoured formation under his command, the veteran 7th Armoured Division, which had been virtually decimated at St Vith during the Battle of the Bulge but which had now been built up again, to launch a reconnaissance in force and make an orderly contact with the Russians.

The dubious honour of crossing the front and facing not only German resistance but also potential trouble with the

1. Prior to the war the German captain had been at Oxford studying the House of Lords.

Russians was given to a recent West Point graduate, First Lieutenant William Knowlton. He was told on orders that presumably came down from Brigadier-General Bruce Clarke, one of the most daring tank commanders in the US Army, that the Russians were 'somewhere to the east—between 50 and 100 miles, according to rumour'. Knowlton's face dropped when he heard the distance; that would take his 90-man force almost to Berlin. But he accepted his lot with good grace along with half-a-dozen bottles of Hennessy cognac that he was to give to the first senior Russian commander he met to persuade him to return with the reconnaissance force to the American lines.

Late on the afternoon of 2 May he set off, with his little force of eleven armoured cars and twenty jeeps strung out behind him, heading north-east. The first German soldiers they encountered simply threw their arms away when they saw the Americans and volunteered to march into captivity without an escort. A few hours later when they drove into the little town of Parchim they were met by cheering throngs of civilians and soldiers lining the sides of the streets six deep. German MPs, machine-pistols slung over their shoulders, held them back and saluted as the dusty armoured cars rolled past. To Knowlton it looked as if the Germans regarded them more as liberators than conquerors. Later he learned that the Germans thought he was driving east to fight the Russians.

But he had no time to stop in Parchim. It was beginning to grow dark and he knew that his thin-skinned armoured cars were at the mercy of any fanatical Hitler Youth with a bazooka. He decided to stop and set up his command post in a *Gasthaus* at the little town of Lübz nine miles east of Parchim.

His day of triumph was not yet over, however. His presence was reported to General von Tippelskirch, the commander of the 200,000-strong 21st German Army, which was retreating before the advancing Russians. The former German intelligence chief realized that this might be the chance to save his Army from Russian captivity. He ordered his staff officers to make contact with Knowlton to see if he would accept the surrender of the 21st Army to the Americans.

That night one of the officers who met Knowlton in the little inn radioed to his divisional commander, Ernst von Jungenfeld, that he had met an 'American captain' who was 'in command of twenty tanks' and that 'both of us tank leaders, with forty good tanks request you personally order an attack against the East, to start the morning of 4 May. We believe that with Hitler dead, it is the moment finally to defeat and crush the Russians and thereby communism. Therefore we request you and expect from you a clear attack order against the East and we are convinced that we will defeat and drive out the Russians and we are also sure that everywhere other comrades will immediately follow our example.'[2]

Back in Wismar trouble had already broken out between the paratroopers and their Soviet Allies. The situation in the town was chaotic. Hundreds of ragged *Wehrmacht* soldiers were wandering the streets wondering how and to whom they were going to surrender. In the main square the bodies of half-a-dozen German civilians dangled from nooses in the bandstand where in former, happier days brass bands had played to promenading crowds. They had fired on British troops. Everywhere the paras were enjoying the fruits of their victory, drinking looted schnapps and staggering off to look for 'Frauleins'.

They were not alone in their search for women. The Russians in their ankle length coats were looking for them too. Some time that evening a score of drunken Russians staggered up to the entrance of the main town hospital. Pushing forward to the British sentry, they cried in broken German, 'Women—we want women.'

The sentry realized that the Russians must have found out that the hospital housed a large number of nurses and female *Wehrmacht* auxiliaries, the 'field mattresses' as the German soldiers called them crudely.

'There's no women here!' he retorted.

The leading Russian pushed his face close to the paratrooper's. The soldier pulled back a pace. 'Here—women,' he said in barely intelligible German. 'We want.'

Other men from the 7th Parachute Battalion who had been enjoying themselves with the German girls appeared at the windows of the hospital. The Russians saw them and made threatening gestures with their weapons, waving about unsteadily in the courtyard. (Later the British found out that the Russians had been drinking V1 fuel mixed with vodka.)

Again they made their drunken demands for 'women'. On the second floor a half-naked para shouted: 'They're our girls. Bugger off!'

The Russians did not understand. But they did the threatening gesture a Red Beret made with his sten. Suddenly a shot rang out. Moments later it was followed by the rattle of a sten. The Russians scattered. Shooting broke out everywhere. It

2. A surprised yet suddenly optimistic Jungenfeld radioed the Americans to try to get confirmation of the strange request, but he failed to make contact.

didn't last long. But when it was over there were six or seven Russians stretched out in the courtyard, dead. The first fight between the erstwhile Allies had taken place.


## II


By mid-afternoon on 2 May, Admiral Dönitz knew that his plans of the day before had come to naught. The Elbe Line had been breached completely. Soon Hamburg would be occupied by the British and the enemy would flood over Schleswig-Holstein. His fears were confirmed a little while later by Lüdde-Neurath who burst into the Admiral's office to explain that he had just been telephoning Lübeck when the officer at the other end had broken off the call with the words: 'British tanks are beginning to pass by!' Lübeck as well as Wismar had fallen now and the British were advancing further north towards Travemünde and the Danish border. He realized that he would have to evacuate his own HQ at Plön before the British overran it. Swiftly he ordered the evacuation and the transfer of the most important offices to Flensburg close to the Danish border. At the same time he telephoned Admiral von Friedeburg and told him to meet the evacuation convoy at the bridge over the *Kaiser Wilhelm Kanal* near Kiel.

The journey was a nightmare. Burning trucks and automobiles, shot up only minutes before by the British *jabos* (fighter-bombers) which were everywhere in their hundreds, dotted the whole road. Twice Dönitz was forced to halt and take refuge from the British Typhoons. But he forced the pace, telling his driver not to have any scruples about pushing boldly and brutally through the mass of civilian and military vehicles which blocked the road.

It was dark when he reached the appointed meeting place at the bridge. But there was no sign of von Friedeburg. An hour passed. Dönitz bit his lip nervously. Had his old comrade been killed in one of the British low-level attacks? What was he going to do now? Where would he find a substitute for the Admiral? The Army staff wouldn't do; he didn't trust them as he did von Friedeburg. Just as he was about to give up and drive away, von Friedeburg's Mercedes rattled across the bridge. Hurriedly he stepped out and explained that he, too, had been delayed by British air attacks and like Dönitz had been forced to take cover more than once. The Grand Admiral waved aside his apologies. Time was running out. Taking him to one side, he told him that time had come for him to go to Montgomery and obtain a truce, or partial surrender or anything which would allow him to slip as many German soldiers and civilians as possible through the 'escape hole' to the West and away from the Russians. 'You must play for time—*time*!'

After von Friedeburg had left on his journey to the south and his death, Dönitz sped towards Flensburg with Schwerin von Krosigk at his side. On the way Dönitz approved a policy speech which the latter wanted to give over the radio immediately they arrived at Flensburg. Krosigk hurried to the local radio station as soon as Dönitz had boarded the SS *Patria*, the ship which was to be his headquarters for the next few days. He stepped up to the mike. 'German men and women.' He began in the style familiar to his listeners after twelve years of Nazi propaganda; he told them about the millions of Germans fleeing from the East. 'The Russians move closer and closer; behind them, hidden from the eyes of the world, all those people caught in the mighty hands of the Bolsheviks are being destroyed.'

He went on to explain that the current San Francisco Conference which was trying to set up the United Nations might bring peace. 'But a Bolshevik Europe,' he predicted would be the first step towards a world revolution planned by Russia for over a quarter of a century. 'Therefore we don't see in San Francisco what an anxious mankind is longing for. And we also believe that a world constitution must be established, not only to prevent further wars but to remove the tinder-boxes which start war. But such a constitution cannot be established if the Red incendiary helps establish it ... The world must now make a decision of the greatest consequence to the history of mankind. Upon that decision depends chaos or order, war or peace, death or life...'

III

The ceasefire in Hamburg came over the air at dawn. But not by trumpet call as in the past. The cavalry of 1945 heard it through the earphones of their tank headsets. 'In Hamburg all resistance has ceased.'

The veterans of six years' fighting in two continents prepared to move in. NCOs rapped out orders. Officers pointed with their sticks. Vehicles were loaded, weapons given a last

106

check. Then as the first light of dawn flushed the sky, the order to 'mount up' was given and the tank engines coughed into life.

In front of the great procession of armoured vehicles came the infantry brigade in its trucks, the soldiers crouching warily in their carriers, rifles and machine-guns held at the ready in case some fanatic started shooting. Behind them came the tanks—scores of them laden with jerricans, bedrolls, spare tracks and the accumulated loot of a year's fighting. They were led by the only two tanks of the Division which had survived the campaign since the 7th had landed in Normandy in June, 1944—*Sharpshooter* and *Jerboa*, the desert rat which had given the Division its name so long ago.

They left the tree-lined surburbs with their nineteenth-century villas behind and saw for the first time the real extent of the damage wrought by the RAF. Whole sections of the town were laid bare: a desert of brick waste, with here and there a ruined wall or shattered chimney stack standing out starkly. Everywhere there were mountainous heaps of twisted metal, girders and rubble. They had seen devastation enough in London, Foggia, Naples, Caen—but never anything like this. To some of them it seemed so bad that they assumed the city would be abandoned after the war. Indeed the damage was so bad that one column got completely lost and had to ask one of the elderly leather-helmeted policemen who were still on duty (two days before they had been fighting the 15th Scottish on the Elbe, but the tankmen did not know that) if he could show the bewildered Britishers the way. Thus the column continued with a somewhat startled German policeman riding on the lead tank.

Colonel Bill Wainman of the Division's reconnaissance regiment the 11th Hussars, the famous 'cherry pickers', was not lost. In the usual manner of his carefree formation he was way ahead of the rest of the Division. Thus it was that he sailed into the *Ratshausplatz* in front of the Gothic town hall to find General Wolz and a host of other bemedalled dignitaries ready to surrender the keys of the city to him. The Germans sprang to attention as the colonel in his GI combat jacket and baggy civilian trousers emerged from his car. But Wainman ignored them. Instead he groped somewhere in the bowels of the vehicle for a packet of army issue biscuits. He crumbled them up and began to feed the crumbs to the pigeons which came soaring down from the high roof as he walked up and down the square sedately making cooing sounds. Finally he acknowledged the group of General Wolz's staff officers waiting rigidly to surrender. One of them spoke English and said they would like to surrender. Colonel Wainman waved him airily aside, saying he'd have to leave 'that job to the brigadier' and went back to feeding his pigeons until the officer in question arrived.

IV

At about the same time that the 7th Armoured Division started its drive into Hamburg, First Lieutenant Knowlton of its American namesake met the Russians. All morning he had been working his way through a minefield with two German officers perched on his armoured car to whom he had said at the outset of his journey, 'Now, gentlemen, if my car hits a mine, you will be just as dead or slightly more so than anyone in the car.'

Then about noon, as they were approaching the little town of Reppetin, one of the Germans perched precariously on the bonnet of the Staghound yelled: '*Da ist unsere Artillerie!*' and pointed ahead at a long line of horse-drawn vehicles. Knowlton studied the column through his glasses. Then he shook his head and handed them to the pale-faced unshaven German. 'Look again,' he commented drily, 'and then tell me how long the German Army has had Cossacks in high fur caps riding with it.'

They were the Russians.

The Russians swarmed around the American vehicles, fingering the US equipment, comparing weapons, drinking toasts, shooting off their weapons (one of them nearly shot his own commander with a burst fired accidentally from the American 50-calibre machine-gun) and shouting their heads off.

The Russians had a fantastic collection of vehicles, ranging from horse-drawn *panje* wagons, looted from some unfortunate Polish farmer months before, to German diesels, wood-burning automobiles of all shapes and sizes—and all filled with a mass of dirty, shouting men and women, their flat yellow faces gleaming with sweat, schnapps and excitement.

Then a colonel appeared. He snapped something to the squat little riflemen, with their tommy guns hanging around their necks and loaves of looted bread thrust in their mud-coloured blouses. A bunch of them swung themselves on their

108

shaggy little horses and galloped off to a large house close by. There was the sound of raised voices. Moments later two Germans shot through the front door. A Russian appeared holding a screaming, struggling boy by the seat of his short pants. Without even a grunt, he threw the boy effortlessly over the nearest hedge. The colonel turned to Knowlton and extending his hand courteously, he invited him into his new headquarters. It was as simple as that.

Meanwhile back at Parchim Tippelskirch's Chief of Staff, Colonel von Varnbuhler, whose intelligence officer Knowlton had seen the night before, had now arranged a meeting between his chief and General Gavin of the 82nd Airborne.

'Slim Jim' received the commander of the 21st Army at the Grand Ducal Palace at Ludwigslust. He ushered him into the echoing Great Hall and bade him sit down under the slightly dusty and creased American flags which now decorated it. Von Tippelskirch got down to business at once. The Russians were at his heels, and there was every indication that Rokossovksy would launch his final attack on the morrow. He felt it his first duty to save his men.

'My soldiers,' he told the airborne commander, 'wouldn't surrender to the Russians. They aren't scared of the Russians as fighters. But they do fear the Russian POW camps. If I ordered my men to surrender unconditionally (Gavin had asked for this) there would be a mass flight to the West. The Russians would follow this up and there'd be a bloodbath among the refugees who are with my troops.'

'What do you suggest then?' Gavin asked.

Tippelskirch licked his lips. 'I must continue the fight against the Russians. I must give my army a chance to retreat to the West. If you allow me to do this, I'll order my troops not to fire a single shot against you and to down their weapons as soon as they reach your lines?'

Gavin shook his head. Did Tippelskirch really think he could accept such terms? After all the Russians were his allies. 'In no circumstances,' he told him 'can we approve your continued fighting on the Eastern Front while we come to an agreement with you behind the Russians' backs.'

In spite of the American's uncompromising answer, General von Tippelskirch refused to give up hope. He racked his brain for some compromise solution that would save his men and the civilians they had brought with them from the East.

'Couldn't we find some formula,' he suggested, 'which leaves the Russians out of it altogether. Let's limit ourselves to an undertaking on my part that I shall order my troops to lay down their weapons immediately they reach your lines?'

Gavin thought it over a few moments. Then he nodded. 'Okay, draw up your suggestion on paper, and I'll see what my superiors have to say about it.'

Von Tippelskirch at once jotted down a couple of sentences and handed the paper to General Gavin. It read: 'The 21st Army is continuing the withdrawal action from the enemy and is preventing Russian breakthroughs. Personnel who encounter the Anglo-American forces in the course of this withdrawal are to stop fighting and to surrender to them, laying down their weapons.' Gavin added a few corrections of his own. Thereafter the conversation was suspended for half an hour while he went to telephone.

Finally Gavin reappeared, smiling slightly. Even before he spoke, Von Tippelskirch knew what the answer would be. The Western Allies had agreed. He had saved his men.

The big surrender could begin—one that General Gavin would later call 'without precedent in American military history'. By that afternoon prisoners were pouring into the divisional cages so fast that it was impossible to keep an exact tally. But intelligence officers estimated that they amounted to at least 150,000 men. As one eyewitness remembers: '(they) rode in Wehrmacht trucks, trailers, tracked vehicles and automobiles. Many others rode in wagons, resting on bundles of hay for their horses. The convoy moved on anything with wheels, bicycles, charcoal-burning and gasoline civilian autos, all manner of carts—ox-drawn, hand-drawn, tractor-drawn ... Many walked until they could walk no further, then flung themselves along the roadside until they recovered strength to push on.'

Gavin's Airborne had made history. A whole enemy army had surrendered to a division of just over 10,000 men. But more important, the surrender of the 21st Army meant the end of Dönitz's hopes of retaining some control over the situation in North-West Germany. His Elbe Line had already gone with the surrender of Hamburg; the British had reached the sea and cut off the escape route; now his rear was wide open to the Russians who would flood westwards into the vacuum created by von Tippleskirch's surrender.[3]

The end had come. It was time for the big surrender.

3. The only effective east–west escape route left open on 3 May was by sea from the Mecklenburg ports not yet taken by the Russians to the many harbours which dotted the Schleswig-Holstein coastline under Dönitz's control.

They came in a Mercedes. In front of them there was a British armoured car preceded by Colonel J. O. Ewart, Montgomery's representative, who had escorted them from Hamburg that morning. As they stepped out of the cars, they presented a perfect caricature of the Nazi officer, complete with jackboots, long belted coats that came down to their ankles and their general air of pent-up defiance.

At 11.30 am precisely they strode across the damp heather to where Montgomery's staff officers were waiting for them. The doomed men—only one of them would survive the next two weeks[4]—strode past the self-propelled gun half hidden in the bushes towards Montgomery's caravan, where the Field-Marshal was waiting for them on the steps. There they lined up on the white mark already prepared for them while Montgomery surveyed them from above.

Then he spoke, 'What do you want?'

'We have come,' von Friedeburg said through the interpreter (they had forgotten to bring their own), 'from Field-Marshal Busch to ask you to accept the surrender of three German armies now withdrawing in front of the Russians in Mecklenburg.'

There was an excited burst of chatter among the correspondents some way off who had already noted that an admiral was doing the talking and correctly concluded that this was more than a local surrender; these men had come from Dönitz himself.

Von Friedeburg looked at the letter which Field-Marshal Keitel had prepared for him the day before and began to read from it : 'We are very anxious about the conditions of German civilians who are being driven along as these armies are fleeing from the advancing Russians.'

Montgomery waited till his tartan-hatted interpreter had put their words into English. Then he said, 'No, certainly not. The armies concerned are fighting the Russians. If they surrender to anybody, it must be to the Russians. Nothing to do with me.' He hesitated and seemed about to turn back into his caravan. The German officers stared at the cold face of the British Field-Marshal. Von Friedeburg bit his lip and tried to hide his feelings. If he had known what had happened earlier at General Gavin's HQ, his mind might have been eased. Nor

4. Of the four men who came to surrender that day, Admiral von Friedeburg was to commit suicide by poison, General Kinzel shot himself, Major Friedel was killed in a motor accident with his British escort. Only Admiral Wagner survived to become deputy head of the Federal German Navy in years to come.

did he know the quandary in which Field-Marshal Montgomery found himself. The latter has never revealed what went through his mind as he stood there on the steps of the caravan which he had looted from the Italians many years before. But we do know that he was well aware that the reinforcement barrel was about scraped clean. Churchill had been forced that spring to take essential skilled workers out of the war industry to refill the gaps in his, Montgomery's, decimated infantry divisions. Every day that passed brought a further weakening of British potential to take offensive action. Further prolonged fighting in Norway and Denmark, which was conceivable if he did not soon make peace with the Jerries (as he liked to call them), was unthinkable. There was still the war with Japan to be won; and at the same time he needed strength in the West to deal with the Russians. The war must be brought to a successful conclusion *now*.

But back in Rheims Eisenhower still stuck doggedly to unconditional surrender, the agreement made with the Russians two years before. To Ike the Russians were pretty much like the Americans: a people (to use Eisenhower's own words) who 'bear a marked similarity to what we call an average American'. Admittedly Eisenhower had told him the day before that he had the freedom to accept a limited surrender—what Eisenhower called 'a tactical manoeuvre', whatever that might mean. But Montgomery wanted the surrender of all the German forces in North-West Europe, those facing both the Western and the Russian Allies. Dare he risk Eisenhower's wrath in making such a demand?

Suddenly he made up his mind. 'Are you prepared to surrender to me the German forces on my western and northern flanks. All forces between Lübeck and Holland and all forces in support of them—such as Denmark.'[5]

Von Friedeburg's reply was instantaneous. '*Nein*'; but the '*nein*' was no longer so confident. Hurriedly he went on. 'We are very anxious indeed about the conditions of civilians in those areas, and we would like to come to some agreement with you whereby they will not be slaughtered. '

This time it was Montgomery's turn to say no. 'I am not

5. The demand naturally could be interpreted as meaning all forces on the eastern bank of the Elbe, i.e. facing the Russians too. Both Montgomery's book *From Normandy to the Baltic* and Lüdde-Neurath's *7 Tage Schattenkabinett Dönitz* lead one to believe that this is what Montgomery really wanted. Rear-Admiral Wagner believes that von Friedeburg wanted the surrender of all German forces both *east* and west of the River Elbe.

going to discuss any conditions with you,' he said coldly. But he did add that he was 'no monster', a phrase the Germans seized upon like drowning men clutching at a straw. Then he remarked, 'I wonder whether any of you know the battle situation on the Western Front?'

They shook their heads and Montgomery had his battle map brought out to display to them the rash of red crayon marks which illustrated the progress of his forces over North-West Germany. As he was to say later: 'It was a great shock to them. They were amazed and very upset.'

Admiral von Friedeburg broke down completely. He burst into tears. Montgomery, who could never stand emotion displayed in public, ordered him and his companions to be taken away and given lunch. The Admiral cried throughout the meal.

An hour later Montgomery ordered them to be brought back to him. As he saw it 'they were in a condition—a good condition, a good ripe condition—to receive a further blow'.

'You must understand clearly,' he said, 'three points. You must surrender to me unconditionally all the German forces in Holland, in Friesland, including the Frisian Islands, in Schleswig-Holstein and in Denmark. Two: Once you have done that I shall be prepared to discuss with you the implications of that surrender—that is how we shall dispose of those forces, our occupation and so on. Accept point one and discuss two. Three: If you don't agree to Number One, I shall go on with the war and will be delighted to do so and all your soldiers and civilians will be killed.'

Von Friedeburg thought the terms of Point One unbearably harsh. It meant an end to Dönitz's plan to stall as long as possible and use the occupied countries as a pawn to achieve better terms. Yet he felt a faint hope well up within him as he considered the second point. It might be interpreted as meaning that the Field-Marshal was not going to take the expression 'unconditional surrender' literally. He answered slowly and thoughtfully. 'We came here entirely for the purpose of asking you to accept the surrender of our armies on your eastern flank. And we have been given powers to agree to that only. We have not power to agree to your demands. Two of us will go back and two will remain until we return.'

Montgomery nodded his agreement and turned back into his caravan.

As he sat down alone and considered what he had done that afternoon, Montgomery knew that the die was cast. He had taken the plunge, without prompting from his staff; without permission from Eisenhower or advice from Churchill he had made an unauthorized decision which might bring the whole war in the west to an end. But at the same time he knew he was taking a tremendous risk. If his decision did not meet with Eisenhower's favour because the Supreme Commander felt that it might offend the Russians—a few days before there had been a tremendous fuss because Alexander had approved a partial surrender of the German forces in Italy[6]—he might lose all the power and prestige that he had won since El Alamein. Eisenhower was so powerful now that he would not hesitate to fire him at once and Churchill would be constrained to support the American. There would be no doubt about that.

Yet if he pulled off this unexpected surrender, he would achieve a great triumph for British arms and overshadow the fact that his army had been relegated to a sideshow since the Rhine crossing, due to Bradley's machinations. He would have the kudos of the final great victory after all—even though it had not taken him to Berlin. It was a risk worth taking.

v

For over a month Montgomery had been depressed, ever since that message from Eisenhower in the last week of March telling him that his Army was to play no more than a flanking role to Bradley for the rest of the war. One of the newest of his 'eyes and ears', Major Howarth, who had come to him from the infantry in February that year had been especially aware of the chief's despair. 'He was moody,' he recalled later. 'Not about little things, but about something big of which we were not aware. He rarely visited our mess as he had done of old and spent the evening chatting to us. He kept very much to himself in those last days.'

But Monty's depression was not occasioned by military considerations alone; in part it had a personal basis. For at that moment of his triumph when victory was within sight, the young man he had depended upon for so long, Major John Poston of the 11th Hussars, had been killed in an absurd little ambush; and there was no one else among his 'eyes and ears' who could replace Poston in his affection.

All his life he had steeled himself against affection ever since his mother had beaten the lesson into him that she had no love

6. Field-Marshal Alexander, in charge of Allied troops in Italy.

for him. He had married late, at forty, and his 'one great love' had been of short duration. She had left him with a son, David, but the boy was too young to solace him in his loss.

When he met Poston in the desert in 1942, the young man had taken the place of the family he had never had; and he was the first of many other brave young men who had won the affection of the 'chief' after earning their laurels on the battle-field.

Now the most senior of his 'eyes and ears' had died the way he had lived: brave, tough and careless of his personal safety. Poston was always discovering short cuts. But on that April day he had discovered one short cut too many. He and Major Earle had driven into a German ambush, manned by a few fanatical German boys. Earle had dropped to the ground, but Poston had driven his jeep straight at them, then shot it out from the ditch into which he swerved. A little later Mont-gomery had followed his coffin to a grave dug in the side of a muddy German field. Then after the platoon of infantry had fired the last volley, he had walked alone to the grave and saluted it. On the same day he had written an uncharacteristic letter to the *Times*, which read:

> There can be few young officers who have seen this war from the inside as did John Poston. He knew everything that was going on and was in possession of much informa-tion that is secret and must remain secret for all time. We trod the path together from Alamein to the Elbe.
>
> I gave him my complete trust and confidence and he would come to me with his own personal troubles. He had been through this war from the beginning and he saw the end approaching. The Promised Land was not so very far away and he gave his life that others might enjoy it.
>
> I was completely devoted to him and I feel very sad.

But now on this afternoon of 4 May his mood of despair had vanished. Admittedly he was still worried what Eisenhower might think of his talk with the Germans on the day before, but if he pulled off the surrender of the German forces in the North-West he would have achieved a greater victory than he ever did in North Africa. A million Germans, or so his intelli-gence officers assured him—might go into the bag, three times as many as at Stalingrad or as had recently surrendered to the Americans in the Ruhr.

It was, therefore, in a mood of elation that he addressed the assembled war correspondents in the big tent that had been put up for them outside his HQ that afternoon. Most of the correspondents, such as Alan Moorhead and R. W. Thompson who had known him for a long time, had never seen him in better form; he sparkled, spluttering out his words 'gaily like a boy'.

'My intention is,' he told his attentive and for once utterly silent listeners, 'that they shall sign a piece of paper I have prepared ... I am dealing with the Command of forces facing me. I am demanding from him complete tactical surrender of forces fighting me. And I have absolutely excluded anything that might be an Allied matter.'

At this moment Montgomery was informed that von Friedeburg was back. He chuckled, 'Ha, he is back! He was to come back with the doings. Now we shall see what the form is.'

But he did not break off his briefing. Instead he chuckled again, 'like a schoolboy', R. W. Thompson thought. 'No doubt that if the piece of paper is signed forces to be surrendered total over a million chaps. Not so bad, a million chaps!' he cried, his bright sharp eyes disappearing into the myriad wrinkles surrounding them. '*Good egg!*' And with that he was gone, leaving the correspondents with that bit of school boy slang. But as Thompson, no admirer of Montgomery's, wrote that day: 'At this moment Montgomery was superb, the complete master of the situation. A conqueror.'

It was six o'clock and getting dark. It was raining and bitterly cold. Fighter planes roared over the North German plain where the German Army had once practised for the victories of the early years of the war. Montgomery emerged from his caravan. He was dressed as informally as ever—duffle coat and black beret. One hand was thrust deep into his pocket and in the other he held 'the piece of paper', on which the fate of so many millions depended. He vanished into the brown tent with its wooden trestle table, covered with a grey army blanket, upon which the surrender would be signed.

Then the Germans came, making their way awkwardly through the springy pot-holed heather to the little hillside. Von Friedeburg in his long grey raincoat led the little procession, escorted by two British staff officers. Behind him came General Kinzel, Admiral Wagner, Major Friedel and Colonel Pollek. The only splash of colour in the whole sombre scene was the bright scarlet of Kinzel's broad general staff officer's lapels. They halted on the white line and waited.

The minutes ticked by. Then they were all ushered into the

116

tent and seated themselves after saluting the Field-Marshal. One of them in his nervousness tried to light a cigarette. Montgomery looked at him. He put it out immediately.

Then Montgomery began to read from the 'piece of paper'. 'The German Command agree to surrender all German forces ... to Commander in Chief Twenty-One Army Group ... All hostilities to cease eight hundred hours British Double Summer Time Fifth of May 1945 ...'

Finally Montgomery looked up. 'The German delegation will now sign. They will sign in order of seniority.' For Thompson, his words 'were like hammer-blows on an anvil, each one dropping into the minds of us all indelibly and into the minds of the Germans like pins of fire in raw wounds'.

'General Admiral von Friedeburg first,' he ordered.

The Admiral rose and with an army-issue pen—which Montgomery commented could 'have been bought in any post office for twopence'—signed rapidly as if he wanted to get the miserable business over with once and for all.[7]

Then Kinzel rose. He bent over the table, and added his signature to the documents. So they followed as Montgomery called their names one by one until the last—Major Friedel. 'And Major Freide,' he said, mispronouncing the young officer's name, 'will sign last.'

Montgomery paused, then raising his voice above the whirr of the newsreel cameras, he said firmly: 'Now I will sign on behalf of the Supreme Allied Commander, General Eisenhower.'

Bending down, his lips hard and set, he signed and added the date. It was the 4th, but he wrote 5. Then he saw his mistake. He crossed out the original, initialled the erasure 'BLM' and wrote '4 May 1945, 1830 hrs'. When he had finished he sighed faintly and sat back in his chair. A moment later he was master of himself again. He removed his glasses and said: 'That concludes the formal surrender.'[8]

They filed out. Montgomery called for the photographer who had snapped the German group as they had approached the tent a few minutes before. 'Did you get that picture—

7. Montgomery refused to surrender the original 'piece of paper' to Eisenhower although ordered to do so. In the end Churchill had to defend Montgomery's right to keep it in the House of Commons. But in 1968 after the Field-Marshal's house had been burgled, his resistance broke; he handed it over to the keeping of the Imperial War Museum in London.

8. Later Montgomery commented: 'I don't know what happened to the pen we all used. I suppose someone pinched it.'

under the Union Jack?' he pointed to the flag flapping above his head.

The photographer said he had.

'Good, good. An historic picture.'

A little while later he saw von Friedeburg for the last time in his caravan. The latter asked what the status of the German High Command in Flensburg would be now, since they were still conducting operations against the Americans and Russians. Montgomery was in a good mood. He cracked one of his rare jokes. Informing the German that with effect 0800 hours the next day the High Command were his prisoner, he added, 'And I cannot allow you to conduct operations against the Russians and Americans after that time.'

Von Friedeburg was in no mood for jokes and he did not respond. As Montgomery chuckled later: 'I do not think the German delegation saw the humour of the situation.'

After the Germans had been escorted away, von Friedeburg remaining at Montgomery's Headquarters prior to leaving for Rheims the following morning, the Field-Marshal had dinner, emerging a little later to inform the correspondents: 'It looks as if the British Empire's part in the German War in Western Europe is over ... I was persuaded to drink some champagne at dinner tonight.' Then he went on his way to his caravan laughing.[9]

For most of the commanders the news of the surrender came in the dry, unemotional officialese of General Belchem, Montgomery's Chief-of-Administration's signal:

9. The next day a simple wooden monument was erected on the site of the surrender on the Timmerlohberg. It read: 'Here on the 4th of May 1945 a delegation from the German High Command surrendered unconditionally to Field Marshal Montgomery all Land, Sea and Air Forces in North-West Germany, Denmark and Holland.' It was stolen a few days later, replaced and stolen again. In the end the British Occupation Authorities told the burgomaster of the nearest village, Wendisch-Evern, that he was responsible for its safety. The frightened burgomaster, a Herr Karl Baisse, took his responsibility seriously and the 15-cwt granite block was never stolen again, but in 1955 unknown Germans wrote on it 'This victory allowed communism to spread to the heart of Europe. Ten years later it is time to recognize the common danger. Let's forget the past.' In 1958 on the occasion of the evacuation of the British garrison from Lüneberg, Montgomery, who was present, was asked if he minded the stone being removed. He said no, if the Germans didn't, and thus today the stone graces Sandhurst, the British officer-training academy.

From: Exfor Main.
To: For Action: First Cdn Army: Second Brit Army L of
C: GHQ AATPS:
   79 Armd Div. Exfor Rear.
For Infm: Second TAF: Exfor TAC: 22 Liaison HQ.
GO 411 A Secret: all offensive ops will cease from receipt
this signal. orders will be given all tps to cease fire 0800 hrs
tomorrow saturday 5 may. full terms of local German surrender arranged today for 21 Army Gp front follow. emphasize these provisions apply solely 21 Army Gp and are for
the moment excl. of Dunkirk.          ACK.
  In cipher if liable to interception      DOP
  R. M. Belchem.                 Emergency

One of Montgomery's key commanders heard the news in a
very strange place. Brian Horrocks, Chief of the victorious
XXX Corps at Bremen remembers: 'I had often wondered
how the war would end. When it came it could hardly have
been more of an anti-climax. I happened to be sitting in the
military equivalent of the smallest room when I heard a voice
on the wireless saying: "All hostilities will cease at 0800 hours
tomorrow morning 5th May." '

Some wouldn't believe the news. General Thomas of Horrocks' 43rd Infantry Division was planning an attack on
Bremerhaven when there was a thunderous knock on the door
of his caravan. Major Chalmers, the Brigade Major, burst in.
The assembled staff officers looked up from the map in surprise. *Nothing* was ever supposed to disturb a briefing—and
everyone in the Division knew that. As one of the staff officers
remembers: 'Even if the news had just come in that God had
decided to come down from heaven and join in the war on our
side, it still wouldn't have been grounds enough to disturb the
General!'

'Sir,' the tall major said, standing with his head bowed at the
low doorway, 'Sir.'

'Well,' Thomas snorted. 'What is it?'

'The BBC have just announced the unconditional surrender
of the German Forces opposing Field-Marshal Montgomery
in North-West Europe,' Chalmers said breathlessly.

Calmly and in silence, the General mustered the other officers, as if he heard news like that every day of the week.

Then he said, 'I take my orders from the Corps Commander
and *not* the BBC!'

Without another word the General bent over his map and
the Major withdrew. Ten minutes passed. Again there was a

knock on the door of the caravan. The back of the General's neck flushed an angry red. 'Come in!' he roared. It was the unfortunate Chalmers again. This time he had a piece of paper in his hand.

'Sir, personal message from the Corps Commander, timed 2115 hours,' he said hurriedly.

'Read it,' Thomas barked.

Clearing his throat the Major read the brief signal ending on 'Hostilities on all Second Army fronts will cease 0800 hours tomorrow fifth May. No repeat ...' Abruptly his voice trailed away as he stared at the General with the rest of the staff officers present following the direction of his gaze.

General Thomas did not seem to understand. His brow was furrowed as if he were thinking hard. Then he slowly pulled the frayed old canvas cover over his map talc for the last time and walked to the door. Silently and thoughtfully Thomas walked to his armoured car with one of his brigadiers. He reached up to get in. Then he stopped and turned to the other man. 'The troops have done us damn well!' he said. Then he got in his vehicle and roared off at full speed up the road, standing upright as if on parade to acknowledge the brigadier's salute.

# 3

# Round-up at the Little Red School House

## 5–8 MAY, 1945

'There is no greater fatuity than a political judgement dressed in a military uniform.'

*Lloyd George*

I

Butcher, the ex-radio executive, who was Eisenhower's public relations man, prepared for the surrender at Rheims as if he were on location in Hollywood. The Map Room on the second floor of the *École Professionelle et Technique des Garçons,* which in peace-time had been used for table tennis and chess, and which was now hung with charts and maps indicating the Allied dispositions, was strewn with batteries of high voltage klieg lights, power cables and camera equipment. Ignoring the guards and the bewildered staff officers, the cameramen had taken over and had pushed the battered schoolroom table, normally in the centre of the room, to the far corner to permit more coverage for their lenses in the dark, blue-painted L-shaped room.

Butcher himself, as he recalls, was 'running around like crazy, taking care of phone calls from Paris, the needs of the photographers' and a score of other major and minor details. On the one hand, he felt, he 'seemed to be an aide of the Supreme Commander, and, on the other, the representative of the world press, radio and movie interests'.

Some time during that Sunday morning while he waited for the arrival of Colonel-General Jodl from Flensburg, Eisenhower himself wandered into the room. He took one look and then went out hastily, muttering that the 'damned room looked like a Hollywood setting!'

Shortly after noon his Chief-of-Staff, General Bedell Smith, came in. He exploded when he saw the place. 'Who represents the PRD[1] here?' he thundered.

1. Public Relations Division.

One of Butcher's men murmured timidly that he 'guessed' he did.

'Then whoever's responsible for all that Hollywood equipment', Bedell Smith shouted, 'must get it out immediately! This isn't going to be a show. There's going to be a surrender. Get it out immediately!'

Bedell Smith and Eisenhower were understandably short-tempered. Neither had slept much during the last two nights and Eisenhower, in particular, was (to use Butcher's words) 'pretty well whipped down from the tension of waiting and interruptions to his sleep caused by the Prime Minister and others telephoning him' during the night.

In addition Eisenhower was worried. Von Friedeburg, who had arrived the day before, had broken down completely and was of no further use in the negotiations; now they were waiting for Jodl to come, but the latter was hours overdue. And if that wasn't bad enough, the Russians were kicking up a fuss about the whole surrender mess. As they saw it, he was trying to make a separate peace with the Germans and they had already protested about the attempts of individual Germans to surrender to the Western Allies but not to the Russians. This was somewhat unfair since Eisenhower had taken great pains to impress upon his commanders in the field that they could only accept limited surrenders and that proposals for more extensive surrenders would have to be submitted to Supreme HQ for acceptance by both himself and by the Russian representative at Rheims, General Suslaparov. In particular, he had warned Montgomery, and as soon as he had heard that Dönitz had approached him, had informed the Russians. He knew Montgomery's and Churchill's attitude to the Soviets and he was not going to allow them to ruin his attempts to secure an understanding with the Russians. But already a message was on its way from Moscow stating that Stalin was not prepared to accept the Rheims surrender or the document of surrender prepared by Bedell Smith.[2]

As the Soviets wrote: 'The Soviet High Command prefers that the signing of the "Act of Military Surrender" take place

2. For some strange reason Bedell Smith forgot that he had in his secret safe the surrender document as prepared by Churchill, Roosevelt and Stalin. Instead he prepared his own. When it was already too late Robert Murphy, Eisenhower's political adviser, told him about it and after Smith had found it, the former remarked: '(He had) suffered a rare lapse of memory.' An unlikely assumption and another of the little mysteries surrounding the great surrender which will never be explained now, as all the chief participants save General Strong are dead.

in Berlin', with Marshal Zhukov, the victor of Berlin, signing for Russia. But fortunately for General Eisenhower the message did not arrive until a day later.[3]


II


Just after five-thirty that afternoon Colonel-General Jodl finally arrived. He was accompanied by Major Wilhelm Oxenius[4] and Montgomery's Chief-of-Staff, General de Guingand. Jodl was taken straight to the little office which had been given to von Friedeburg. All he said as he closed the door behind him was 'ah-ha', but an American member of Butcher's staff peering in through the keyhole noted that he didn't salute the pale-faced shaken Admiral.

Moments later an aide came out asking for coffee and 'a map of Europe'. His wish was granted and the man at the keyhole could see Jodl pacing up and down in the room, coffee cup in hand while he talked urgently and rapidly to the Admiral. Like everyone else that Sunday Jodl was agitated and nervous, although he did not show it like von Friedeburg. Indeed, in spite of the fact he had not slept much over the last three nights, his uniform was spotless and well-pressed and he had all his facts at his finger-tips.

Yet his appearance and behaviour were deceptive. Jodl was about at the end of his tether. For years he had lived in the artificial atmosphere of Hitler's HQ, avoiding political decisions, concerning himself with the strategic and tactical policy-making at which he excelled. Now he was confronted with the knowledge that the decisions made over the map board that day meant life or death for countless thousands of human beings.

In his pocket he bore Dönitz's written instructions which read:

> Try once again to explain the reasons why we wish to make this separate surrender to the Americans. If you have no more success with Eisenhower than Friedeburg had, offer

3. Again another of the 'little mysteries'; why should such a vitally important message take so long to arrive?
4. After the war Major Oxenius served in the London Embassy of the Federal Republic and sent his son to St Paul's School, Monty's old public school. The headmaster was ex-Major Howarth, one of Monty's 'eyes and ears'.

a simultaneous surrender *on all fronts,* to be implemented in two phases. During the first phase all hostilities will have ceased, but the German troops will still be allowed liberty of movement. During the second phase this liberty will be withheld. Try and make the interval before the introduction of Phase Two as long as possible and, if you can, get Eisenhower to agree that individual German soldiers will in any case be allowed to surrender to the Americans. The greater your success in these directions, the greater will be the number of German soldiers and refugees who will find salvation in the west.

Dönitz had also given him power of attorney to sign the surrender for all the surviving fronts, but had warned him 'Use this authorization only if you find that your first object of separate surrender cannot be reached' and only after he had received radio confirmation from the Admiral himself. In other words he was (*a*) to try to convince the Americans that the German Army should be allowed to continue to fight the Russians for as long as possible or failing that (*b*) gain as much time as he could squeeze out of the enemy. The stakes were high, perhaps 'a couple of million German soldiers and civilians', as Dönitz had said.

Five years before at the French surrender negotiations at Compiègne Jodl had told the French General Huntzinger, who had protested against the harshness of the German surrender terms, '(all he could do was) to give explanations and clear up obscure points'; the French would have to take the armistice document as it was or leave it. Now he was no longer in a position to limit himself just to 'give explanations and clear up obscure points'. Today it was his task to fight for time and concessions in any way he knew with the knowledge that to a certain extent, the future of the German Nation depended upon his ability as a negotiator.

There was a soft knock on the door, and Oxenius opened it. It was General Strong, Eisenhower's British Chief-of-Intelligence. In fluent German—he had been British military attaché to Berlin prior to the war—he told the Germans that General Bedell Smith was waiting for Jodl to begin the surrender negotiations. Jodl rose, pulled down his cuffs, and followed the British General from the room.

Bedell Smith got down to business at once, with General Strong doing the interpreting, and at once he was obliged to reappraise his attitude to General Jodl. He had been led to believe from von Friedeburg that Jodl would sign the surrender right away. He was wrong. Jodl was prepared to do nothing of the sort. As General Strong remembers, 'he told us frankly and with deep conviction that we would soon find ourselves fighting Russia and that if Germany were given time to evacuate as many troops and civilians as possible to the West there would be then large resources available to help the Allies in their struggle against the Russians.'

Smith listened patiently. Then he said, 'You have played for high stakes. When we crossed the Rhine you had lost the war. Yet you continued to hope for discord among the Allies. That discord has not come. I am in no position to help you out of the difficulties that have grown out of this policy of yours. I have to maintain the existing agreements among the Allies.'

Like Eisenhower, Bedell Smith believed firmly that the future lay in the hands of Russia and America. As he told Strong when they parted at the end of the war, 'Britain is old-fashioned and out of date.' The countries of the future were Russia and the United States and they must remain Allies now the war was over. So he rejected Jodl's statement as the usual German attempt to spread trouble between the Eastern and Western Allies.

Jodl then put forward his two-stage plan. Again Smith listened politely, then said he'd have to put the idea to Eisenhower. He went out and returned almost at once. Eisenhower said that the surrender must be completed at once. Looking straight at Jodl he said, 'If you decline, the discussions will be considered closed. You will have to deal with the Russians alone. Our Air Force will resume operations. Our lines will be closed even to individual German soldiers and civilians. I don't understand why you don't want to surrender to our Russian allies. It would be the best thing to do for all concerned.'

One doesn't know what went through Jodl's head at the moment when Strong translated Smith's words. They must have struck him as the height of naïvety or the bitterest of sarcasm; but he pulled himself together and replied, 'Even if you are right, I should not be able to convince a single German that you are.'

It was getting late. Most of the staff officers had gone home to bed, convinced that there would be no surrender that night. Only the correspondents still hung around the 'little red schoolhouse' hoping for a story. Eisenhower himself had gone to a WAC[5] cocktail party, run by Captain Summersby. One of the Russians of Susloparov's group tried to drink American

5. The female auxiliary of the US Army.

125

rye like vodka and left, with the rest of the Soviet officers, exceedingly rapidly. Eisenhower stayed a few minutes only, 'his thoughts far away from the cocktail chatter' (as Kay Summersby wrote later). He left saying to her: 'Kay, keep in touch with the office. Let me know what's happening.'

At the school General Strong, acutely aware that 'men were still being killed', tried a new tack. He suggested to Smith that a tradionalist like Jodl would fall for a 'soldier-to-soldier' approach. He reminded him of the importance that the Germans attached 'to honour and prestige' in the Army and suggested he should play upon this. Smith agreed to have a try.

The new line worked well. Jodl listened attentively to Smith's long speech, made with an absolutely straight face, and 'showing a fine understanding of German mentality' (as Strong wrote later) though he wasn't sure 'to what extent Bedell Smith believed anything of what he had said'. In the end Jodl asked if he could discuss the matter with von Friedeburg, and this was agreed.

Jodl came back an hour later. He had drafted a message to Dönitz recommending capitulation, in which he had included, almost verbatim, Smith's statement about the prestige and honour of the German Army. When the American saw it, he exploded. 'Tear the damn thing up,' he told Strong, 'and tell Jodl that it can never be sent in its present form.'[6]

Jodl now made a strong plea for a further delay, as the breakdown of the communications system of the German Armed Forces made it impossible to contact all units within the next few hours. Strong got on the telephone to Eisenhower and recommended that he agree to Jodl's request. The Supreme Commander agreed, telling Strong he must inform Jodl that, 'You can tell them that forty-eight hours from midnight tonight, I will close my lines on the Western Front so no more Germans can get through. Whether they sign or not—no matter how much time they take.'

Strong passed the message to Smith who handed it on to Jodl, adding, 'If you decline, the discussions will be closed.' He gave the German half an hour to think it over.

Jodl did not need the time. He stood up and said, 'I shall send a message to Marshal Keitel by radio. It is to read—We sign or general chaos.'

6. It never was. But Strong kept a copy which he wanted to present to Bedell Smith as a souvenir. The latter told him gruffly to destroy it and all other copies. They were.

126

At one o'clock in the morning Jodl's message arrived at Dönitz's HQ. It read:

Eisenhower insists that we sign today. If not, the Allied fronts will be closed to persons seeking to surrender individually, and all negotiations will be broken off. I see no alternative—chaos or signature. I ask you to confirm to me immediately by radio that I have full powers to sign capitulation. Capitulation will then come into effect. Hostilities will then cease at midnight German summer time, 9 May.[7]

Dönitz's hand shook as he read the message. The Eisenhower demand was 'sheer extortion', he muttered, his breath taken away by the harshness of the American terms.

Back in Rheims Jodl was frantic with worry. Three hours had gone by since he had sent the radio message to Dönitz and still he had received no reply. The German High Command radio system had obviously broken down. When midnight passed without a reply, Jodl called a German signals officer left behind at Montgomery's HQ at Lüneburg and shouted down the telephone, 'You must get through to Dönitz at all costs. *We've got to get an answer tonight!'* After three decades of trying to hide his true personality behind the code of conduct of the professional German soldier, Jodl was beginning to crack.

It was around 0200 and the HQ was awake again. Kay Summersby telephoned Eisenhower, but he was already on his way back from his Château. So she hurried to the school, where brilliant klieg lights blazed in the Map Room in preparation. In his own room Eisenhower was pacing back and forth, out of his office into Kay's and then back again. For the moment he had no role to play. At his own command he was to take no part in the surrender until Jodl had signed 'on the dotted line'. As a result 'the atmosphere was electric with his impatience' as Kay Summersby wrote later. Though 'at the same time, I thought it rather lonely and pathetic in the Supreme Commander's office. The silence was heavy with the contrast to the bustle in the War Room.'

Jodl, fresh and shaven, now knew that it was all over. The long awaited message had at last come through. It was so dis-

7. i.e. midnight 8/9 May, 1945.

torted that it was virtually unintelligible. '*I* can understand it,' the German liaison officer had said. 'It says that Dönitz agrees.'

'Will you take the responsibility of advising General Jodl to that effect?' an Allied officer asked.

The German agreed and hurried off to see General Jodl. The long wait was over.

The room was full of correspondents, cameramen and photographers when the Allied officers entered. General Spaatz joked with General Ivan Susloparov, the Russian representative who was never seen again after he left for Berlin the next day.[8]

At two-thirty General Bedell Smith entered, followed two minutes later by General Strong who informed him that the Germans had arrived. Smith said curtly, 'Bring them in.'

Friedeburg came in first, his face expressionless. Jodl and Oxenius followed. When they were in the room Jodl took up his place between the other two and after bowing the three of them sat down facing the Allied officers. There was a slight pause while Strong took his place at their side, ready to translate. For the top Allied intelligence man this was a personal triumph. Before the war Keitel had once told him that military attachés were a 'bunch of military idlers'. Now he, the military idler, was in essence running the whole show, giving his support to Smith and advising Eisenhower that this second surrender should be arranged so that no German legend of another 'stab in the back' could arise, as after 1918. This time the Germans would *know* that their senior officers had surrendered to the victorious allies. They wouldn't be able to place the blame on anyone else but themselves.

While the cameramen darted all over the room, climbing ladders and standing on chairs, the surrender document was passed from allied representative to allied representative for signature. Then it was Jodl's turn. The German's face was impassive as he signed. Only Friedeburg seemed disturbed by the commotion and the constant flashing of the cameras.

At 0246 hours Smith rose and spoke a few words to Jodl. No one could hear them. They may have been a question, asking him if he had anything to say. Whatever they were, they occasioned the most dramatic moment of the surrender when, after signing with a flourish, Jodl said in English, 'General, with this

8. For some reason he incurred Stalin's displeasure and General Strong writes: 'From the moment he stepped out of one of our aeroplanes at Tempelhof (Berlin) we never saw him again; any enquiries we made about him were received with blank faces.'

signature the German people and the German armed forces are, for better or for worse, delivered into the victors' hands.'

He then lapsed into German which Strong translated awkwardly. 'In this war which has lasted more than five years both have achieved and suffered more than perhaps any other people in the world. In this hour I can only express the hope that the victor will treat them with generosity.' Jodl appeared on the verge of tears. He regained his composure, however, and watched the Allied generals' faces for some reaction. There was none. Smith simply nodded his head. The rest sat in silence. Jodl's head dropped in defeat. His hands were trembling violently.

Kay Summersby sitting in the outer office heard the heavy tread of their boots as they came along the corridor. She looked up and saw Jodl led by Strong and followed by Oxenius and von Friedeburg. She rose from her desk in respect, but the thought crossed her mind that the Germans looked 'exact prototypes of film-land Nazis, sour-faced, glum and despicable'.

Eisenhower was waiting for them 'more military than I had ever seen him'. 'Do you understand the terms of the document of surrender you have just signed?' he asked. Strong interpreted and the Germans answered, '*Ja.*'

'You will get details of instructions at a later date. And you will be expected to carry them out faithfully.'

Jodl nodded. Then Eisenhower said, 'You will be held officially and personally responsible if the terms of the surrender are violated, including its provision for the German commanders to appear in Berlin at the moment set by the Russian High Command to accomplish a formal surrender to that Government. That is all.'

Jodl said nothing. He saluted and turned.

Moments after Jodl had left, General Susloparov led the Russian officers into General Eisenhower's office. He grasped Eisenhower's hand firmly and the latter beamed. 'This is a great moment for all of us,' Eisenhower said.


IV


In London when the news of the surrender was released on Tuesday morning, Major Desmond Morton was summoned to Churchill's bedroom. The great man was still in bed and on the counterpane were strewn the typed foolscap sheets of the victory speech he had been working on all Monday; it would be the last speech of his wartime premiership. He was tired, but putting on his big black spectacles he asked Morton to listen while he rehearsed. Morton, who was perhaps the most 'personal' of Churchill's personal staff, said that it was perfect but suggested diffidently that such a soulful performance needed some reference to the Almighty.

Churchill grinned. 'Desmond,' he said, 'in a few hours' time I go to the House of Commons and inform those members present that the war with Germany is over; an hour or so later I go on the wireless and tell the people of these islands that the war with Germany is over; at three o'clock this afternoon, in company with the legislators of this realm, I go to St Margaret's, Westminster, and tell Almighty God that the war with Germany is over!'

But there was no humour in the speech which Churchill broadcast that day. After remarking that 'I wish I could tell you tonight that all our toils and troubles were over. Then indeed I could end my five years' service happily, and if you thought that you had had enough of me and that I ought to be put out to grass I would take it with the best of grace,' he continued. 'On the continent of Europe we have yet to make sure that the simple and honourable purposes for which we entered the war are not brushed aside or overlooked in the months following our successes and that the words "freedom", "democracy" and "liberation" are not distorted from their true meaning as we have understood them. There would be little use in punishing the Hitlerites for their crimes if law and justice did not rule, and if totalitarian or police Governments were to take the place of the German invaders. We seek nothing for ourselves. But we must make sure that those causes which we fought for find recognition at the peace table in facts as well as words, and above all we must labour to ensure that the World Organization which the United Nations are creating at San Francisco does not become an idle name, does not become a shield for the strong and a mockery for the weak. It is the victors who must search their hearts in their glowing hours and be worthy by their nobility of the immense forces that they wield.'

Dönitz, in faraway Flensburg, struck an equally dismal note in his address to the beaten German people that day. 'Comrades ... We have been set back for a thousand years in our history. Land that was German for a thousand years has now fallen into Russian hands. Therefore the political line we must follow is very plain. It is clear that we have to go along with the Western Powers and work with them in the occupied territories in the west, for it is only through working with them that we can have hopes of later retrieving our land from the Russians...

'The personal fate of each of us is uncertain. That, however, is unimportant. What is important is that we maintain at the highest level the comradeship amongst us that was created through the bombing attacks on our country. Only through this unity will it be possible for us to master the coming difficult times and only in this manner can we be sure that the German people will not die.'

# III

## END OF AN EMPIRE

'War's hell, but peacetime'll kill you!'
*Old Soldiers' Saying*

# I

# The Rebels
## 8–10 MAY, 1945

'I intend to hold out here with you until the Fatherland
has won back its lost ground.'

*Admiral Huffmeier,*
*May, 1945*

I

On the evening of Friday, 28 June, 1940, long queues of
trucks, horse-drawn carts and vans lined up along the White
Rock Quay, Guernsey in the Channel Islands, waiting to unload their cargoes of 'chips', as the twelve-pound baskets of
tomatoes are called, into the holds of the waiting British
freighters. It was a fine evening and the farmers, although
British, chatted in the local French patois as they enjoyed the
summer sun and waited for their turn to unload their tomatoes for the British market. The war seemed a long way off
that evening.

Then abruptly at five minutes to seven, six planes flashed
into sight. Three of them roared high into the sky and flew
across the island from east to west. The other three lost height
and roared towards the waiting farmers. A farmer recognized
the insignia. '*Jerries!*' he yelled, using the English word. They
could see the swastika and iron cross quite plainly. Then the
machine-guns started to chatter. The crowd panicked. Some
threw themselves under the trucks. Others scrambled under
the pier, throwing themselves flat in the shingle. A few jumped
into the sea.

Before they were aware of what had happened the planes
were gone. But behind them they left a confused mess of dead
and dying civilians, their blood mingling with the red pulp of
their squashed tomatoes, once Guernsey's pride. The Germans
had arrived in the Channel Islands.

That month they had arrived at a dozen similar ports and
harbours ranging from Lorient in the western French prov-
ince of Brittany to the Dutch island of Texel in the north.

They had dug themselves in as if they were going to stay for ever. At first they had been content to establish their military headquarters, take over barracks and occupy hospitals for their sick and wounded. But as the weeks gave way to months and the months to years, they began to make themselves comfortable. *Die Etappenhengste,* the 'rear echelon stallions', as the front-line troops called them contemptuously, arrived and opened clubs: cinemas were requisitioned, brothels set up. Local contractors were hired to supply them with services—plumbers, electricians, carpenters, men offering every kind of service. A black market sprang up in everything from silk stockings to postage stamps. And then there were the girls—French, Belgian, Dutch—and British.

It was no different in the only part of the British Isles to be occupied by the Germans in World War II. In the Channel Islands the years that followed were strange ones. There were plenty of hardships naturally. Foodstuffs in this one-time land of plenty were hard to obtain. By 1944 that British 'essential'—tea—cost £28[1] a pound and a bar of soap ten shillings. But the Islanders had their cricket and football matches as of old, complete with 'fixtures' against their German occupiers. There were dances too, behind locked doors because dances were not allowed, to the sounds of the latest British tunes taken from the BBC. By 1942 the VD rate had risen so alarmingly that the authorities were forced to publish an order stating that 'Sexual relations either with the German soldiers or with civilians are strictly forbidden during the next three months. In case of non-compliance with this Order severe punishment by the Occupying Authorities is to be expected even if no infection takes place.'[2]

But if by 1944 the food situation of the Islanders was bad, that of the 30,000 occupying Germans, who called themselves *Division Kanada,* believing that to be their final destination, was no better—in fact, in many cases it was worse. Their fuel supplies had given out. Their rations were cut to 1,125 calories a day. Tuberculosis reached epidemic proportions, and the military doctors estimated that only 5 per cent of the men were capable of combat. The starved soldiers waylaid civilians and stole their Red Cross parcels—to be shot out of hand by the 'chain dogs' if they were caught. In that year the starved, dis-

1. At the 1944 rate of exchange—$120.
2. In the end the Germans were forced to open brothels with French girls who got 'heavy workers' rations' for their services. The brothels were divided into those intended for 'other ranks' and those 'for officers only'; even in bed 'rank hath its privileges'.

10 *British troops crossing the Elbe in assault craft, 29 April, 1945.*

11 *Field-Marshal Montgomery accepts the surrender of the German armed forces on Luneburg Heath, 3 May, 1945. Nearest to him is Admiral von Frie who committed suicide two weeks later.*

12 *Captain Loladze, officer in charge of the Russian battalion which mutinied on the island of Texel, and fought on three weeks after the war had officially ended.*

13 *Some of the survivors of the 800 mutineers just before they were shipped back to Russia. 25 May, 1945.*

contented German soldiery formed an underground organization to force their commanders to surrender to the British as soon as possible.

By this time the war had passed by the Channel Islands and the rest of the coastal fortifications on the French and Dutch mainland. As the Allies had driven deeper into France they paused to take these fortresses, but the bloody capture of Brest which had cost Bradley 10,000 casualties for what he called a 'prestige object' had been a lesson to them. They decided to contain these outposts with second-class troops and those of their Allies who were not up to front-line combat, such as the French and the Czechs. So they were left—Texel, Dunkirk, Lorient and the Channel Islands, plus a dozen smaller ports, officially designated *'Festungen'* (fortresses) by Hitler and commanded by tough admirals and generals, totally devoted to the Nazi cause.

Now as the war was ending these *'Festungen'* were becoming a dangerous embarrassment to Dönitz in faraway Flensburg as he tried to preserve the newly-won peace and his tenuous authority in the Flensburg Enclave, still not yet occupied by the British.

Problem number one among these fortress commanders was Admiral Huffmeier, commander of the German forces on the Channel Islands. The tough, forty-six-year-old sailor who had once been commandant on board the German battleship *Scharnhorst* was such a fanatical last-ditch fighter that his men called him the 'madman of the Channel Islands' and had twice tried to murder him.[3] But Huffmeier was not a man who gave up easily and he paid no attention to what his men thought of him—as long as he could get them to fight. And the events of the past few weeks had shown that even the starved and sickly *Division Kanada* could still fight when the occasion demanded.

On 9 March, 1945, the day that the American 9th Armoured Division captured the famous Remagen Bridge across the Rhine, Huffmeier, 500 miles behind the front, had launched one of the most audacious commando raids of the war; he had sent his men to capture the French port of Granville, once Eisenhower's first HQ in France, now a quiet backwater of the war.

Lt-Commander Sandel in the US *PC 564*, an American torpedo boat, had been the first to spot the German convoy as it

3. Once they had tried to entice him away with a female decoy—the Admiral had an eye for a pretty girl. The plan was to kidnap him and ship him to England and then surrender. But the scheme failed.

swung up the Channel. The young naval officer had only taken over command a few days before and his crew was a scratch one, recruited mainly from US port offices in England. But he didn't hesitate. As soon as the first suspicious green blobs appeared on the radar screen he set course for the Germans.

He saw them when they were 3 miles away. Immediately he ordered three flares shot into the air for identification purposes. But even before he could identify the suspicious shapes, a German flare burst directly above his ship, bathing it in an icy white light. His response was immediate.

'Open fire!' he yelled to the gun crew under Lt Klinger. Klinger roared a command. The 76-mm cracked into action. The little ship shuddered. But the shell hit the water 200 yards away from the leading enemy ship.

Klinger yelled 'fire' again. Nothing happened. The brand-new artillery piece had jammed after the first round!

The torpedo boat didn't get a second chance. With a roar the more powerful German 88 opened up. The shell hit the bridge, killing or wounding everyone on it. Sandel and Klinger fell to the deck, bleeding heavily and seriously wounded.

A moment later another shell landed directly on the torpedo boat's second piece, a 4-cm cannon. It sprang apart. Two further shells followed, striking the *PC 564* like a great metallic fist, so that it reeled in the water under the impact. Drifting helplessly, its steering gone, its radio and radar knocked out, the little ship disappeared into the night leaving the field to the Germans, overjoyed at the first success in their daring venture.

The Germans took the little port by complete surprise. A French infantry company, commanded by a Captain St Amand, alarmed by the noise of the Germans landing, got out of their bunks. But their CO ordered them back to their quarters. Later, when asked why, the Frenchman shrugged and said, 'I thought the Americans were out on night manoeuvres and everybody knows that *they* do things completely different to the rest of the world.'

Thus while the French defence company went back to sleep, the Germans swarmed ashore. The English port officer Lt Lightholder was felled by a burst of machine-gun fire as he ran to his jeep to sound the alarm. The port commander, American Lt-Commander Diefenbach, ran for help but could find no one to help him.

The German engineers, working against time as they wanted to be at sea again before dawn, blew up installations throughout the supply port, cheering every time a crane or loading device came crashing down.

Meanwhile the infantry of *Division Kanada* swept through the town freeing their own men who were working for the Allies in the docks, jubilantly herding Allied officers, some still in their night clothes, out of their hotels at bayonet point and everywhere cramming anything edible down their starved throats. The unique and audacious raid 500 miles behind the battlefront went without a hitch. The Germans took a hundred prisoners, released fifty-five of their own men, blew up four ships and captured one British coaler complete with crew. When the first American Sherman crawled cautiously into the port just before dawn, it found the birds flown and the docks a smouldering shambles.

A few days later Admiral Huffmeier held a parade at which he awarded the Iron Cross to several members of the raiding party who had distinguished themselves. This he followed up with something more welcome than the piece of metal—a packet of cigarettes and a jar of looted jam for each man.

Huffmeier's example caught on. At Dunkirk, where the defences were virtually impregnable from the sea, Admiral Frisius, who was in charge of the 12,000-strong garrison, launched his own attack. Under the code 'Operation Blücher', he sent a specially trained company under a Major Turke to attack the Allied troops surrounding the port, who were commanded by the Czech General Miska. Turke caught the Allies completely off guard. While British tanks rolled into Lübeck, British engineers at Gravelines, 10 miles south of Dunkirk, blew the bridge across the River Aa in the face of the surprise attack while over eighty-nine Czechs wandered into the triumphant Germans' POW cage!

All along the coastline Allied troops reported attacks by German forces, real or imaginary, and while in Germany itself the front-line soldiers celebrated their imminent victory, their second-line comrades dug themselves in and prepared for further German commando attacks.

With good reason too, since Huffmeier had decided to attack the mainland once again to boost the sinking morale of *Division Kanada*. He reasoned that if the Americans thought he would attack them, as he anticipated he would, they'd expect him everywhere bar one place—*Granville*! Therefore, why not launch a second commando raid against the French port, but this time one which would finish it off for good?

A few days before, he had assembled the key figures in his

command in the Forum Picture House and told them that he would not allow the Channel Islands to fall into enemy hands. Raising his voice so used to shouting above North Sea gales, he had cried out, 'I intend to hold out here with you until the Fatherland has won back its lost ground and the final victory is wrested from the enemy. We do not wish, and we cannot allow ourselves, to be shamed by the Fatherland!'

The response had been lukewarm. His starving audience, living off nettle soup and boiled potatoes, knew the war was already lost. Grimly he had looked down at them and concluded in a harsh determined voice, 'As Commander of the defences of the Channel Islands, I will carry out without compromise the mandate given me by the Fuhrer. We stand by him, officers and men of the Fortress of Jersey!'

Shocked by the lack of enthusiasm shown by his officers and key personnel, he had decided that the raid must take place soon in order to raise morale. Ordering Lt-Commander Zimmermann to his office he gave him his instructions. Carefully Zimmermann noted down his orders. Under the command of a Lt Meyer, a group of volunteers would be segregated from the rest of *Division Kanada*, fed the best food available and then given the task of blocking the harbour at Granville with a large freighter filled with cement. Thereafter they would escape the best they could to a waiting Luftwaffe high-speed rescue boat.

Huffmeier looked at the young man. 'Any questions?'

'The date, sir?'

'The seventh of May.'

II

Dönitz's problems with his remaining outposts, cut off from Flensburg by many hundred miles of enemy occupied territory,[4] were not limited to the Channel area. On the Dutch island of Texel, the small flat island situated opposite the important naval base of Den Helder, a full-scale miniature war had been under way since the end of April. At that time the island had been garrisoned by the 822nd Infantry Battalion, a mixed force made up of 800 Russians from Soviet Georgia, who had volunteered to serve in the German Army after being

4. Up to the end there was radio contact with his HQ and the occasional torpedo boats which managed to sneak through the Allied net.

taken prisoner, and about 400 German officers and NCOs. But with the end of the war in sight the Georgians lost confidence in their German masters; they feared that they might be thrown into some last-ditch battle by the fanatical commander of what remained of German-occupied Holland.

So they established contact with the local Dutch communist underground, who fed the unhappy Georgians resistance literature urging them not to work for the fascists. The Georgians decided there was only one way out—mutiny.

The man they picked to lead them was Lt Sjalwa Loladze, a former Air Force pilot, who after being shot down had survived the German death camps by 'volunteering' for the *Wehrmacht*. To support him they picked Sergeant Eugene Artemidze, the Battalion's Political Commissar, who was the brains behind the mutiny. According to his way of thinking, if the Russians could seize the Island, complete with its artillery batteries they would be able to hold out against the Germans, ten minutes away on the mainland, until the British dropped paratroopers to help them. All they needed was to take their German officers and NCOs by surprise and gain the support of the local Dutch populace. By early April, 1945, all 800 Russians had agreed to join in the mutiny.

As the old village clock high up in the brick steeple of Den Burg, Texel's main village, struck midnight, the Russians began to creep out of the billets they shared with the Germans. Silently they crept through the deserted, blacked-out cobbled streets of the village to the prearranged spots where their leaders were waiting for them. In hushed voices they were given their instructions, then they broke up into small groups ready to begin the deadly operation they had planned. Their 'night of the long knives' was about to start.

All over the village and in the outlying billets silent figures sneaked cautiously into the houses occupied by the unsuspecting Germans. They crept up the creaking wooden stairs, entered the tiny bedrooms, heavy with the smell of sleeping men. A grunt. A stifled scream, the long dying intake of breath, and the Russians would emerge as silently as they had come, wiping the bloody knives on the thick grey serge of their uniforms.

Everywhere the mutineers were successful. By morning 250 Germans were murdered and most of the rest were terrified, half-naked prisoners in Russian hands.

But Loladze had two strokes of bad luck. Major Breitner, the 822nd's commander could not be found in his quarters. The Russians looked for him all through the night and finally

141

concluded he was on the mainland somewhere. He was not. He was sleeping with his mistress, in spite of the fact that affairs with local girls were severely frowned upon at HQ. The shooting startled him out of the Dutch girl's arms. For a moment he thought the British had landed. Then he recognized the sound of the weapons being used—they were all German—and realized what was going on. Leaving his mistress behind, he slipped, half-dressed, out of a back window and fled to the shore. At pistol point he forced one of the local fishermen to row him across to the mainland. A few minutes later an excited, dishevelled Breitner was telling the naval commander of Den Helder his story.

The second stroke of bad luck which was to turn the mutiny into a bloodbath was the fact that the Georgians had been unable to capture the German gun batteries which protected the island's boathouse and harbour. With these still in their hands the Germans would be able to land troops from the mainland without interference from the mutineers.

But on the morning after the mutiny Loladze was too elated by his victory to be over concerned with such trivialities. Hastily he set about organizing the defence of the island. He broadcast an appeal for the local people to join him and about one hundred men responded. Then he asked for volunteers from the fishermen to run the gauntlet of the German patrol boats to take some of his men to England, who would ask the English to drop paratroopers to help him. A crew was speedily found and the rescue boat *Joan Hodson* crept by the German batteries that same night set on a course for Cromer, 200 miles away.

His preparations finished, Loladze and his men, now in control of virtually the whole island relaxed and enjoyed the fruits of their victory, dancing with their Dutch girl-friends and drinking the weak local beer and strong Dutch gin.

The following day the mutineers' high spirits were abruptly deflated. Just after midday there was a crump of heavy guns on the mainland. The Russians ran for the protection of their foxholes and concrete bunkers. Minutes later the uncaptured battery on the island joined in the bombardment. It went on all afternoon, raking the whole southern half of the island. Scores of mutineers and many of the inhabitants were killed or wounded, and Burg was transformed into a smoking ruin.

Then, as abruptly as it had started, the bombardment stopped. The shaken Russians who now crawled out of their foxholes soon found out why. The Germans had successfully landed a party of sailors and marines under the cover of the bombardment and already they were beginning to slip into the outskirts of Burg. They dodged from ruin to ruin, taking up their positions for an all out assault.

Loladze reacted quickly. Pushing his men into defensive positions, he prepared to fight back. He was just in time. The Germans came rushing up the cobbled main street, now littered with debris. '*Fire!*' yelled Loladze. From the ruins on both sides of the road, the Russians opened a ragged fire. The German attack fizzled out rapidly. The sailors and marines retreated leaving a score of still figures behind them on the cobbles.

An hour later they attacked again, but not so boldly this time. They advanced down the street under cover of an ancient Mark IV which they had somehow managed to land. The Russians had no antitank weapon. Their positions started to crumble. Reluctantly Loladze ordered a fighting withdrawal while one lone Russian machine-gunner held off the Germans from the local pissoir.

In the days that followed Loladze was forced to retreat further and further into the countryside to the north of the island. But he wasn't without his successes. His men lured a German patrol into a minefield. The Russians knew the island like the backs of their hands. The Germans didn't. One after another they stumbled on the deadly prongs in the morning mist until the field was littered with their shattered bodies.

But Loladze was taking severe casualties too. Faced now by three and a half German battalions, some 3,500 men armed with mortars, he fought back with the surviving 400 Russians. He realized that he could not tackle the enemy as a united command. So he split the survivors up into three groups, one under himself, one under Lt Gongladze and one under Lt Melikia, with orders to carry out guerrilla warfare against the Germans. The three groups would keep contact through runners from the Dutch underground and through the local civilian telephone system using their own language which the Germans didn't understand.

That had been in late April. Now the war on the mainland was over but on Texel the battle still raged, a battle in which no prisoners were taken. When the Germans captured a Russian they made him strip off his uniform and shot him on the spot. The Russians, for their part, were even simpler in their method of 'elimination'. They tied a group of prisoners together and attached a single grenade to them. Then they pulled out the pin and ran. It was their way of saving ammunition.

Meanwhile the *Joan Hodson* had arrived in England. The Russians, according to their own statement were 'arrested by the English and locked up. This cunning trick of the British Government gave one food for thought. We had risen against the Hitlerite occupiers and we had come for help. Instead we were imprisoned!'

The British naturally took them for turncoats and traitors. But the Russians did not know that; they contacted General Rakov of the Soviet Military Mission in London and told him of the desperate need for some kind of support for hard-pressed Loladze. But the British had no parachutists available for that kind of operation; they were all needed for the occupation of Norway.

Thus the fight continued in the dunes and barns of the tiny island, making yet another headache for the hard pressed 'Head of State' in Flensburg.

### III

In his headquarters at the Navy barracks in Mürwik just outside Flensburg, guarded by his own U-boat crews and with the German Naval Cross still flying proudly over the old red-brick building, an enclave in the middle of the British Army, Admiral Dönitz was not enjoying the first day of peace. Both Generals Böhme in Norway and Lindemann in Denmark had shown themselves unwilling to co-operate with the British, while Jodl, his chief military adviser, was inclined to try to play the Anglo-Americans off against the Russians and was no longer much use to him in his anti-Russian course. In the outposts of what was left of the battered Third Reich from the Aegean to the Baltic the local commanders seemingly were not prepared to accept his orders without discussion.

If that were not serious enough, mutiny and dissention were breaking within his own immediate command. On the morning of the previous day, for instance, he had been informed by his staff that an SS unit dug in in the forest near Segeberg had refused to surrender to the British. Hastily he had ordered the local commander to work out some sort of plan to make them surrender with his British opposite number. The two officers, British and German, enemies of the day before, had quickly worked out a plan of action. While the 3rd Royal Tanks and the Somerset Light Infantry had thrown a cordon around the forest, German paratroopers of the 8th Para Division had gone to locate the men. Half an hour passed and then came the well-known, high-pitched burr of a Spandau, followed moments later by another, answering the SS challenge. While British soldiers waited and listened, German fought German.

On that morning of 9 May, Dönitz was equally worried by indiscipline in his own branch of the service. In 1918 the German Navy had been the centre of the revolution which had led to the fall of the Monarchy and he did not want his beloved *Kriegsmarine* to undergo that terrible fate once again. Besides the Navy was the only sizeable force at his immediate command manned by capable officers and NCOs. It was a bargaining counter of importance, he thought, with the Allies. He could not allow it to be demoralized by desertions, discussion —or worse—mutiny. On that day he ordered that any offence of this nature should be punished severely—if necessary by summary execution. He did not have to wait long for the first executions.

On the same day that he issued the order Minesweeper *M 612* sailed into Flensburg. The sullen crew did not have long to wait for the trouble they knew was waiting for them there. Hardly had they tied up when Lt-Commander Reinhart Ostertag came bounding up the heavy wooden gangplank. He exchanged a few hasty words with the boat's skipper, Lt Kropp, and then he turned to glance at the young seamen in their dirty white fatigues, crowding the lower deck.

Nine days before he had told them and the rest of his flotilla, 'In spite of everything, we are going to carry on fighting. Now we're the Free Corps Dönitz.' But the sailors did not share his point of view. They had mutinied, imprisoned their officers and taken over the ship. Now his temper got the better of him. 'Get off the ship!' he roared. 'The German Navy does not go to sea with mutineers!'

At last the thing which Dönitz feared most had come—the rot had reached the vessels of the German Navy.

The 'mutiny', if it can be called that in the fullest sense of the word, had started on the early afternoon of 4 May. That afternoon the *M 612* was anchored off the Danish harbour of Sonderborg when Lt Kropp had called his young crew together and told them he was about to sail for the Hela Peninsula, where many Germans were still trapped. He had received no order to do this—indeed Montgomery had strictly forbidden any such rescue attempts at Lüneburg. Thus it was that when the crew dismissed afterwards there were angry murmurings against the captain; after all the day before he had promised them that they were 'going home'. To add to their anger they heard that the skipper of the *M 601* had told Kropp to stop 'this rubbish' and sail home—a statement that was supported by the jeers of the *M 601*'s crew who cried, 'Don't do it! Our skipper is taking us home! The war's over. You'll never get back alive!' Seeing the looks on the faces of his men, Kropp thereupon ordered his second-in-command Lt Helmut Süss to get rid of the most unreliable elements in the crew before the ship sailed. This done, the *M 612* steamed for Fredericia in North Denmark to take on coal for the trip.

But the boat never left Fredericia. That night the men went ashore and got drunk. Under the leadership of teenage Heinrich Glasmacher, a Catholic from the Rhineland who had volunteered for the Navy, they discussed their situation. As Glasmacher told them, 'It'll be the end of us. It would be better to sail out to the open sea and surrender to the British, or simply land somewhere along the Baltic and abandon the ship.'

The radio operator reported that the Skipper intended to sail at eight-thirty the following morning. Within minutes twenty of the young sailors had volunteered to join Glasmacher in seizing the ship.

It was a very polite mutiny. Glasmacher approached Kropp, pistol in hand and said, 'Herr Leutnant, in the name of the crew we want to go home. It's no use any more.' To gain time he invited Glasmacher to come down to his cabin. But as he entered the door was locked behind him and the other officers arrested. Now Glasmacher took over as skipper while Leading Seaman Wilkowski accepted the rudder. Telling the ones who had joined them that they should 'not worry. The war's over now anyway,' Glasmacher set course for Sonderborg.

The minesweeper didn't get far. Two torpedo boats suddenly appeared, speeding in from each side. Someone had betrayed them. The commandant of the leading boat hailed them through his megaphone and demanded to know why there were armed men on the bridge and where were their officers? Boldly the mutineers yelled back: 'We've had enough!'

'Don't be fools,' the skipper roared back. 'Be good chaps and turn back.'

The mutineers hesitated. Some were for making for open sea in spite of the torpedo boats' guns, but Glasmacher pacified them. Nothing would happen to them now. The war was over, wasn't it?

But as they followed the two other ships into the Als Sund, they suddenly realized they had sailed into a trap. The torpedo boat mothership *Hermann von Wissmann* was waiting for them, her heavy guns trained on the little minesweeper.

After that everything took place with terrifying rapidity. The mutineers were driven off with blows from a boarding party's rifle-butts. A little while later they were summoned before a court martial where they were 'defended' against the charge of 'military rebellion' by a Corporal Weyers. The 'trial' lasted exactly one hour and when it ended eleven of the twenty accused were sentenced to death.

The severity of the verdict was later explained by the Captain who confirmed the sentence, Hugo Pahl. 'All of us, from lowest to the highest rank, were then of the opinion that we were going to fight together with the Western powers against the East. That was our only chance against the Communists. That was Dönitz's great aim too. It was our last chance to stop communism.'

Close to midnight the crew were paraded in front of the bridge. From the rear deck the boarding party covered them with machine-guns. Before them the six men of the firing squad lined up under the command of an officer. Two by two the men to be shot were brought up from below. Heavily laden in chains they were ordered to the bow which was illuminated by searchlights. The officer in charge called his firing squad to attention. The first two to be shot shook hands, embraced and waved to the crew.

'Ready, take aim,' the officer's words rang out. 'AIM! FIRE!'

The shots rang out. The two young mutineers slumped to the deck. The officer rapped out an order. The firing squad relaxed. Those of the mutineers who had been given prison sentences hurried forward to swill their dead friends' blood away.

'Two of us,' Hans Doring, one of those men, remembers, 'were detailed to tie weights—part of a torpedo—on the legs of the dead men and throw them overboard. Three or four of them were shot in the neck by the officer when the doctor didn't think they were quite dead. I remember that Nuckelt had had three salvoes fired at him. But still he didn't die. He groaned and moaned like an animal that had been wounded during the hunt.'

The last man to die was Glasmacher. The guards pushed him and he fell on the blood-slippy deck. Then he drew himself up to his full height, his youthful face very pale but composed. Just before he was killed by German bullets, he cried out at the top of his voice, *'Long live Germany!'*

147

Up and down his command Dönitz's senior naval officers tried to implement his policy of maintaining discipline in the Navy by the strictest of measures. Any historian of that period will come across the details of a handful of sailors shot here, a handful there, days after the war had ended. But nothing in the bitter records of these men's efforts to keep the *Kriegsmarine* under control surpasses the strange story of what took place in German-occupied Amsterdam in that second week in May. There two other German sailors faced a court martial in the echoing ex-Ford factory now filled with some 3,000 German sailors. The two men stared at the high-ranking officers seated at the swastika-draped table and answered their names: Radio Operator Bruno Dorfer, aged twenty, and Leading Machinist Rainer Beck, aged twenty-eight. Then the trial began—and an extraordinary trial it was too; for the spectators, the judges and the accused had been prisoners of the Canadian Army for three days now—and one of the men these fanatical sea officers were trying was half-Jewish.

Bruno Dorfer, a young Austrian, had deserted the Navy at the end of the war and had gone to live with his aunt in Amsterdam; he was sick of the whole mess. Rainer Beck, on the other hand, had been on the run for over eight months for completely different reasons. Beck was the son of a high-ranking police official and war hero, who had been kicked out of the police because he had refused to divorce his Jewish wife. His spirit unbroken, he had threatened to put on his decorations and earn his keep by 'fiddling in the streets' when the Nazis had refused to pay him his pension. However, in 1938 he died and young Rainer had taken refuge in the Navy thinking that there his Jewish origin would be forgotten. But while he was fighting loyally for his Führer, local air-raid wardens were thrusting his sister into the street during raids because they could not tolerate the 'Jewess Beck' in their shelters. Often when Rainer came home on leave he told his sister, 'I am wearing the uniform of the people who want to destroy us.'

In September, 1944, he had had enough. He deserted to the Dutch Underground and hid out in Amsterdam until the day the Canadians marched in when he joyfully surrendered himself to them. But his joy was short-lived. They imprisoned him in a camp full of SS and Gestapo men and he broke out taking Dorfer with him. Two days later he tried again. This time the

Canadians placed him and Dorfer in the Ford camp. Camp Commandant Captain Alexander Stein asked the Canadians to remove them. The Canadians refused and, according to Stein, a Canadian General asked him to court martial the 'two deserters'. One day later Stein convened a court under Staff Judge Wilhelm Köhn. Throughout the whole trial Beck did not speak one word. He heard the sentence of death without any apparent emotion. Perhaps the years of persecution had conditioned him to expect that this was the way that everything must end. And Köhn didn't hesitate. He ordered the sentence to be carried out immediately, remarking later that he didn't believe 'it could conceivably be carried out'.

He was mistaken. A short while later a Canadian truck arrived with captured German Army rifles for the German Navy firing squad. As Köhn maintained later, 'The whole business was occasioned by the Canadian commander. The Canadians organized everything and even told us where the site of the execution would be.'

Later that day the two sailors were led out to the range at Schellingwoude near Amsterdam. There the firing squad was waiting for them. With due ceremony Bruno Dorfer and Rainer Beck were placed with their backs to a brick wall.

At 17.40 pm precisely the officer in charge of the firing squad gave the order to fire. Both men were hit, but only the Austrian died at once. The squad reloaded. Rainer Beck, bleeding from the corner of his mouth, was propped up against the wall again. Five minutes later another volley rang out. The Canadian officer, who was there as an official observer, saluted his German 'colleague'.

v

But Dönitz's measures began to pay off. The Navy settled down. There were no more mutinies, no more desertions. His strict command to the generals and admirals in charge of the outlying 'fortresses' that they would answer for an infringement of the surrender negotiations had its effect.

In Lorient the elderly General Fahrmbacher knew he would have to surrender after nearly a year of defiant resistance to the French and American troops surrounding the port. He called his chief quartermaster and asked, 'How many railway sleepers have we left?'

The man replied, 'One.'

149

Fahrmbacher, who in these last months had even organized company strength raids to bring food into the former U-boat base knew that this was the end; most of the bread, which was the staple diet of his troops, was made up of sawdust obtained from the sleepers of the French railway which had run through Lorient. It was time to surrender. Sending a last radio message to Dönitz on the afternoon of 10 May, which stated, 'Wish to sign off with my steadfast and unbeaten men. We remember our sorely tried homeland. Long live Germany!' he ordered one of his officers to make contact with the French besiegers.[5]

On that same day Loladze, leader of the Russian rebels on Texel was trapped with nine of his men in a lonely farmhouse on the bare dunes to the north of the island. Setting fire to the straw roof of the farm, the German infantry waited for the mutineers to emerge. A machine-gun opened up as they rushed from the door and the Russians fell in a bloody heap before they had gone 5 yards. But Loladze was cooler-headed than his men. When he heard the rattle of the machine-gun, he realized what was happening, and instead of rushing out after them, he ran back and hid in the cellar of the old farmhouse. That night he endured the fearsome heat as the building burned down about him.

Towards morning he crept cautiously up the stone steps of the cellar, pushed his way through the blackened smouldering wooden beams which had collapsed into what had once been the kitchen and looked outside carefully. All was silent. The Germans had gone.

Taking a deep breath and wiping the sweat off his brow, he stepped out into the open. Behind him a twig snapped loudly. He swung round. Too late! He just had time to catch a glimpse of a grey uniform. A second later the burst of machine-gun fire caught him full in the stomach.[6]

In the end the 'madman' gave in too. Huffmeier realized at last that there was no sense in going on fighting.

On the first day of 'peace' two British warships, the *Beagle*

5. The elderly General was to spend five years in a Paris jail because he had 'disfigured French property'. He had overprinted French postage stamps with the word 'Lorient'. Today stamps of this issue are worth £400 each.

6. But the fight on Texel did not end with Loladze's death. Melikia took over until finally the Canadians landed in the third week of May. By then there were only 200 Russians left alive out of the original 800.

and the *Bulldog* made landfall off St Peter Port, Guernsey. They contained Admiral Stuart and Brigadier Snow, the two men responsible for reoccupying the Channel Islands. After some delay the two of them saw an ancient trawler crawling out to meet them, flying the German naval flag. Eventually coming within hailing distance of the immaculate British ships, the decrepit coal-burner heaved to and lowered a much-patched rubber dingy containing two figures in uniform and rowed by several ratings in shabby fatigues. Looking alarmingly as if it were going to sink at any moment, the dinghy finally reached the *Bulldog* and a drenched bedraggled young naval officer clambered on to the spotless desk, splashing sea-water everywhere.

It was Lt-Commander Zimmermann, the planner of the Granville operation, who was now to be Huffmeier's spokesman. His drenched, chinless appearance plus his youth and low rank made no impression on the senior British officers, who regarded the 'whole performance' as an insult to them. But they kept their tempers and waited to hear what he had to say.

Zimmermann demanded to hear the terms of the 'armistice', as he called it, so that he could 'communicate them to his superiors for their consideration'.

Brigadier Snow flushed a choleric purple. He told the German he had come to take the island's 'surrender, not to discuss terms'.

The German who had been living off nettle and turnip-top soup these last few weeks looked at the Englishman's bulk with scarcely veiled contempt. 'I'm to tell you,' he said carefully, 'that you and your continued presence here will be regarded as an unfriendly act.' He looked pointedly at the batteries of heavy guns across the bay. 'Admiral Huffmeier will regard your presence as a breach of faith and a provocative act.'

Snow wasn't impressed. 'Tell Admiral Huffmeier,' he growled, 'that if he opens fire on us we will hang him tomorrow.'

But the British took the hint all the same and after arranging a time for a further meeting sailed away.

Next day the *Bulldog* appeared at the new rendezvous. Again the ancient trawler made its appearance. This time when the young German sailor appeared over the side of the British ship he was accompanied by General Heine, bitterly hated by both Germans and Britons on the islands. But this time the Germans were subdued and polite. The General produced a letter from Huffmeier which indicated that he was afraid that an attempt might be made on his life on the island. It read in part: 'I allowed the English population to fly flags and hold religious services and had therefore to foresee that a certain agitation might be created among my soldiers. This has happened. I was and am therefore not in a position to meet you personally.'

Huffmeier was scared to venture out of his heavily guarded HQ! He had given in.

Two hours later men of the Hampshire Regiment landed in brilliant sunshine while surly Gestapo men in their ankle-length leather coats lurked at the edge of the cheering crowds. The Channel Islands were British once more. The recriminations would soon begin.

Thus by the end of the second week in May Dönitz had quelled all indiscipline within the immediate control of his Flensburg headquarters and at the same time managed to convince the individualistic generals and admirals commanding the 'fortresses' that all further resistance to the Western Allies was useless. By naked force at the lowest level and veiled but effective threats at the highest he had managed to put his own house in order.

But what would happen when the Allied Control Team, led by an American, arrived in Flensburg? Would he be able to cope with them so easily, especially as his own anti-Russian attitude conflicted so patently with that of the Americans? As von Krosigk told him, his only hope was Churchill. But how powerful would the Prime Minister be against Eisenhower's opposition? That he simply did not know.

14 *Petty Officer Beck, who was executed for desertion by the Germans after the war had ended. The execution was carried out with Canadian weapons and approval, and questions were asked about the incident in the Canadian press as recently as 1968.*

15 *Leading Seaman Glasmacher, who was shot for mutiny and thrown over the side of his ship in chains three days after the war had ended. He is now regarded as an anti-fascist hero in the German Democratic Republic, and a minesweeper bears his name.*

16 *Troops of the 52nd Reconnaissance Regiment proudly displaying a captured German flag after the fall of Bremen, April, 1945.*

17 *Members of the German Government arrested by British troops at Admiral Doenitz's HQ in Flensburg, 23 May, 1945.*

18 *The Hotel Palace at Mondorf in Luxemburg where the high-ranking Nazis, including Speer, Goering and Doenitz, were held after the war. The American troops nicknamed it 'Camp Ashcan'.*

# 2

# Failure in London

## 12–22 MAY, 1945

'It would be open to the Russians in a very short time to advance ... to the waters of the North Sea and the Atlantic.'
*Winston Churchill*

I

On 12 May Winston Churchill sent a long, carefully worded telegram to the President of the United States. It read: 'I am profoundly concerned about the European situation. I learn that half the American Air Force in Europe has already begun to move to the Pacific theatre. The newspapers are full of the great movements of the American armies out of Europe. Our armies also are, under previous arrangement, likely to undergo a marked reduction. The Canadian Army will certainly leave. The French are weak and difficult to deal with. Anyone can see that in a very short space of time our armed forces on the Continent will have vanished, except for moderate forces to hold down Germany.

'Meanwhile what is to happen about Russia? ... What will be the position in a year or two, when the British and American Armies have melted and the French has not yet been formed on any major scale, when we have a handful of divisions, mostly French, and when Russia may choose to keep two or three hundred on active service?

'An iron curtain is drawn down upon their front. We do not know what is going on behind ...

'Meanwhile the attention of our peoples will be occupied in inflicting severities upon Germany, which is ruined and prostrate, and it would be open to the Russians in a very short time to advance, if they chose, to the waters of the North Sea and the Atlantic ...'

This famous 'iron curtain'[1] telegram reveals the Prime Min-

1. Churchill did not invent the term as some people think. That doubtful honour seems to go to Goebbels.

ister's desperate attempts that May to prevent any further Russian inroads into West Germany. As he had written to his Foreign Office the month before: 'This war would never have come unless, under American and modernizing pressure, we had driven the Habsburgs out of Austria and Hungary and the Hohenzollerns out of Germany. By making these vacuums we gave the opening for the Hitlerite monster to crawl out of its sewer on to the vacant thrones.' Although, as he said himself, 'these views are very unfashionable' he was determined that West Germany should not become another vacuum into which another monster, a red one this time, should crawl out of its particular sewer.

But time was running out. Soon he would be faced with a general election and although he had won the war for the country he loved so much he was not too sanguine about the influence of the 'khaki vote' on his political future. However, the situation on the 'home front' was not, at that moment, his major concern; it was the problem of the Continent. Eisenhower, in his opinion, was playing right into the Russian hands. Since he had made his famous Elbe decision two months before, he had done nothing, in Churchill's opinion, but give in to the Russians on one occasion after another.

In these last days Churchill had fought desperately to retain his forces. On the 9th he had cabled Eisenhower that 'I have heard with concern that the Germans are to destroy all their aircraft *in situ*. I hope that this policy will not be adopted in regard to weapons and other forms of equipment. We may have great need of these some day and even now they might be of use, both in France and especially in Italy. I think we ought to keep everything worth keeping. The heavy cannon I preserved from the last war fired constantly from the heights of Dover in this war.'[2]

Thus while London was still in the midst of its victory celebrations with each mean bombed backstreet enjoying its 'victory party' drinking its weak beer and dancing between the narrow confines of the red-brick terrace houses, with the paper cross-strips of the anti-blast device still on the windows, Churchill, after six years of war was already haunted by the spectre of a third world war. And to prevent it, he needed American support to keep the Russians as far east as possible and a

2. Even as late as 23 July he was writing to General Ismay: 'What is being done with German rifles? It is a great mistake to destroy rifles. If possible at least a couple of million should be preserved for Britain.'

strong German government—such as that of the anti-Soviet Dönitz—in the west.

In Washington President Truman felt himself obliged to carry out Roosevelt's instructions and his policy of trusting the Soviet leaders. It was a policy which had the approval of most of his advisers, who had survived from the Roosevelt era. In addition most of them distrusted Churchill. Harry Hopkins, for instance, felt that it was vitally important that the United States should not be manoeuvred into a position where she would appear to be lined up with Britain 'as a bloc against Russia to implement England's European policy'. There were many like Hopkins in Washington that May—and not only in Washington but also in Marshall's Pentagon and Eisenhower's Rheims Supreme Headquarters. Churchill's plans to involve America in an anti-Russian bloc in favour of Dönitz and a strong Western occupation Germany could not help but come to naught.

II

The showdown between the Prime Minister and the future President which brought about the end of the former's plans for a strong Western Occupied Germany came about innocently enough. One day before Churchill had sent his 'iron curtain' telegram to Truman, Field-Marshal Busch had announced in his unthinking manner over Radio Flensburg that 'I have taken over command in Schleswig-Holstein and the area occupied by the troops of Field-Marshal Montgomery at the order of Grand Admiral Dönitz and with the agreement of the British occupation authorities. My order gives me the power to be responsible for law and discipline as well as feeding the military and civilian population. I expect unconditional fulfilment of duty and obedience in respect of my orders and prompt co-operation from every individual in the fulfilment of the tasks given to me.'

When Montgomery's intelligence men heard the broadcast they informed the Field-Marshal at once. Busch made it appear that Dönitz was the man giving orders, not the 'Chief'. Montgomery who had just returned from a visit to the Russians at Wismar, a visit which made him note in his diary that 'out of the impact of the Asiatics on the European culture, a new Europe has been born', and occasioned him to order a standstill in the destruction of German weapons 'in case they

155

might be needed by the Western Allies for any reason', commanded Busch to come to his HQ at once.

The Field-Marshal received the ageing German standing, the latter being forced to toe a whitewashed line 3 feet away. Busch was, as Montgomery put it, 'to be put on the carpet'.

After returning Busch's salute, Montgomery told him, 'I only need your staff and you as long as the capitulation is carried out smoothly. If you don't carry out my orders promptly and accordingly, I'll get rid of you and select another officer to take over your job. At the worst the British Army could take over the job. But that would only lead to a delay which could lead to a worsening of the suffering of the German people. After all you've got to see that the German Army was decisively defeated in the field and that you've got to accept the results of that defeat now.'

With that he dismissed him and noted 'After this I had no more trouble with Busch.'

But the Busch affair did not end there. On 13 May *The Times* got hold of the incident and wrote : 'Busch, it will be noted, claims to be acting on the "orders" of Dönitz but only "in agreement" with the British authorities. In the area in which he is affecting to control only one writ runs and that is British. A view widely held is that in usurping power in this way Döntiz and Busch are already seeking to establish a régime with which the Allies will have to deal ... This incident reinforces the need for the earliest disclosure of Allied policy in Germany.' It was a protest that was supported by many other British and Allied newspapers. John MacCormack of the *New York Times* wrote on the same day : 'Recognition of Busch's authority would confirm Dönitz's leadership upon which it depends.' The *Daily Express* protested that a member of a 'military hierarchy' which 'we vowed to destroy' had been given 'renewed prestige and authority by Hitler's successor'. And in Russia Boris Yefimov, top cartoonist of the *Red Star*, drew a cartoon depicting a group of German generals and businessmen sheltering very much at their ease under a large sunshade bearing the legend 'northern military zone'.

In San Francisco, the British Foreign Minister Anthony Eden, alarmed by the mounting American criticism of the 'Busch affair', wrote to Churchill expressing his concern. He was worried, he wrote, that the British attitude might have 'far-reaching constitutional problems' and that the Busch business indicated power was being consolidated in Dönitz's hands which might endanger the major Allied war aim of 'unconditional surrender'.

Churchill replied immediately. His letter illustrated his completely realistic attitude to Dönitz. 'It is of high importance,' he wrote, 'that the surrender of the German people should be completed through agencies which have authority over them. I neither know nor care about Dönitz. He may be a war criminal. He used submarines to sink ships, though with nothing like the success of the First Sea Lord or Admiral King. The question is, has he any power to get the Germans to lay down their arms and hand them over quickly without any more loss of life? We cannot go running around every German slum and argue with every German that it is his duty to surrender or we will shoot him. There must be some kind of force which will give orders which they will obey ...

'I deprecate the raising of these grave constitutional issues at a time when the only question is to avoid sheer chaos. You seem startled at General Busch giving orders. The orders seem to be to get the Germans to do exactly what we want them to do ... In a few days, when we have arrived at solutions to more important questions *requiring action and possibly gun-fire*[3] we will find a great many things will settle down.'

In his final paragraph, he rammed home his intentions brutally: 'It must of course be remembered that if Dönitz is a useful tool to us that will be written off against his war atrocities for being in command of the submarines. Do you want to have a handle with which to manipulate this conquered people, or just to have to thrust your hands into an agitated ant-heap?'

III

Montgomery was first to arrive in London. He had come to spend a leave with Major Reynolds of Hindhead School, the man who looked after his son David during the holidays. He had also arrived with the firm intention 'to impress on the Prime Minister the urgent need for a decision' on the future organization and political control of the British Zone of Occupation.

He was followed a day later by Patton, who had come to be honoured in the British capital before flying to the United States for further honours. Like Montgomery, he was also worried about the future of Germany. The day before, he had been

3. My italics.

in Paris to receive a decoration from General De Gaulle. Sitting in the Hotel Majestic with a bunch of his cronies he had left them in no doubt as to his views on the situation in Germany. Pointing his cigar at them, he had growled 'It's all a God-damned shame. That's what it is.'

Someone asked what was a shame. 'I'll tell you,' said Patton. 'Day after day, some poor bloody Czech or Austrian or Hungarian, even German officers, come into my headquarters. I almost have to keep them from going down on their knees to me. With tears in their eyes they say, "In the name of God, General, come with your Army the rest of the way into our country. Give us a chance to set up our own governments. Give us this last chance to live before it's too late—before the Russians make us slaves for ever." That's what they tell me, and every damned one of them has offered to fight under my flag and bring their men with them. Hell, a German general offered his entire air force, the Third, to fight the Russians if necessary! I'll tell you this; the Third Army alone, with very little other help and with damned few casualties, could lick what's left of the Russians in six weeks. You mark my words. Don't ever forget them. Some day we'll have to fight them and it will take six years and cost us six million lives.'

But his two superior officers, who were soon to get rid of the outspoken, pro-German, anti-Russian Patton, did not think that way when they flew into London on Tuesday the 15th. The two men, Bradley, who was to stay at the Dorchester and also receive British honours, and Eisenhower, who would return for the last time to his wartime 'retreat' Telegraph Cottage in the country some twenty-five minutes[4] from London, firmly believed that they could handle the Russians and that they had to make concessions in order to retain their friendship in the post-war world.

Things had changed greatly since Eisenhower had brought his troops to Europe in the summer of 1942 and he had first encountered the smell of boiled cabbage and Brussels sprouts which seemed a permanent feature of his HQ at 20 Grosvenor Square. Then the Americans had been the 'new boys' who had to suffer the British jokes about being 'overpaid, over-fed, over-sexed—and *over here*'. But as more and more GIs poured into an island which was held up solely 'by the barrage balloons' as they cracked, the American attitude changed. He was now a member of the A.E.F. (American Expeditionary Force) which

4. Near Richmond Park.

stood for 'After England Failed'. In an island only a little larger than Colorado two million of them lived in relative luxury among a people who were underfed and over-worked, shocked by raids and the thousand scares and alarms of the third year of war.

The soldiers began to look down at their hosts. They had the money and the girls were easy—even for the segregated coloured soldiers. England was quaint, but that was about all. They, the Americans, were going to carry the main burden of the invasion—after all they were fielding three divisions for every one in Montgomery's army. When they sailed for France even the most cynical of them felt themselves a little like crusaders, out to save Europe from the 'Nazi jackboot', in the phrase of the time, and 'to bail England out of the mess she had gotten herself in'.

Admittedly Eisenhower did not feel like this. He did not share the opinion of some of his men that Churchill was a secretive old man whose major objective was to promote the interests of the British Empire. Yet he shared in many ways the ordinary American infantryman's black and white attitude to the war and its purpose. For him, the plain dealer, who liked to emphasize his simple Abilene childhood, one had to take a moral stand about its issues. Unlike Churchill and Montgomery who were fighting on their own doorstep and in their own backyard in a desperate attempt to survive so that morality was an unnecessary ballast, Eisenhower could still see things in terms of good and evil. And now in this spring of victory Eisenhower could afford to indulge in his simple ethic; he was all-powerful, supported to the hilt by Truman and Marshall back in Washington and in charge of the greatest Army the United States had ever fielded in all its history—4,000,000 men spread over Western Europe.

That evening Eisenhower, Kay and the rest of his party celebrated. It was their private victory party. Together with General Bradley they all went—after champagne—to see *Strike a New Note* at a London theatre.

In his smart new summer uniform the General looked, according to Kay Summersby, 'boyishly happy', as he took his seat in the box at the Prince of Wales Theatre. The audience went wild when they spotted 'Ike'. They rose to their feet and cheered with un-British abandon. Again, according to Kay Summersby, 'they cheered, whistled, stomped and applauded' until, bowing to cries of 'Speech', he leaned over the rail and signalled them to be quiet with his raised arms.

Briefly, a huge grin on his face, he told them it was a great pleasure to be in the United Kingdom. "It's nice,' he grinned, 'to be back in a country where I can *almost* speak the language.'

The audience loved it. So did the huge group of people who had assembled outside the Prince of Wales Theatre to see him depart and 'merely wanted to see General Eisenhower, perhaps to touch him'.[5]

So they went on to dance into the small hours of the morning at Ciro's night club, the one occasion in his whole wartime career when Kay saw him 'completely relaxed, thoroughly enjoying himself, without a care or a wrinkle of worry'.

Thus they met—Eisenhower, Montgomery and Churchill—for the very last time at the height of their respective power and in their great wartime roles: Eisenhower, Supreme Commander and future President of the United States, who wanted to clear up the 'German mess' quickly so that he could get back home and avoid the criticism that certainly would be levelled at him if he remained in Germany and tried to run a zone like Montgomery was going to do. Churchill, worried and anxious as never before, already conscious the socialists would no longer co-operate with him in the wartime coalition government and that he would soon have to declare a general election; yet at the same time desperately trying to establish a West German barrier to Russia. And Montgomery, that 'gadfly' of the Allied establishment, for whom the knives were already being sharpened: a man 'doomed to seek self-destruction, as if he had a death wish: a man made to be misunderstood'.[6]

Their meeting took place on the morning of 16 May. We do not know exactly what was decided at the two-hour discussion. It is still secret, but the bird-watching Chief of the British Army, Sir Alan Brooke, notes in his diary that '*We did absolutely nothing*! Winston wandered from the number of calories required by German prisoners to Clemmie's[7] experiences in Russia, back to Tito's aspirations in Venezia Giulia, to dash rapidly off into questions of Inter-Allied Control of Germany, back to Clemmie's lunch party in Moscow when all the Moscow ladies had to be provided with dresses by the State, etc., etc.' For the utterly worn-out Brooke, whom Churchill often drove to despair by his hours and methods of work, it was all too much. He shut his ears to the talk and later could recall

5. Kay Summersby: '*Eisenhower was my Boss*' (Dell).
6. Ronald Lewin: *Montgomery* (Batsford).
7. His wife had just returned from Russia.

only that Churchill had uttered a 'series of good catch words' such as 'When the eagles are silent the parrots begin to jabber' and 'Let the Germans find all the mines they have buried and dig them up. Why should they not? Pigs are used to find olives.'

Brooke reminded him politely that pigs were not used to hunt olives, but the interruption did not put the Premier off. He went on to quote a verse he had heard from Clemmie which she said was taught to Soviet schoolchildren. It ran:

*'I love Lenin*
*Lenin was poor, therefore I love poverty*
*Lenin went hungry, therefore I can go hungry.*
*Lenin was often cold, therefore I shall not ask for warmth.'*

The Prime Minister beamed when he had finished the recital and concluded that this was 'Christianity with a tomahawk'. But there was no joy in Churchill's heart and his lack of concentration might be explained by the fact that Eisenhower had already indicated that there was no future for the Dönitz Administration when he had met the Prime Minister briefly the day before. That afternoon his deputy, General Clay, the man who was going to take over the American Zone of Occupation, would tell the Press, with Eisenhower's approval, that 'Dönitz, like Goering, is now held as a prisoner', and give an assurance that General Eisenhower had 'a firm and realistic policy towards the Germans'; Dönitz and the rest were not going to be treated as 'friendly enemies'.

Thus when they parted that afternoon, Eisenhower, briefed by Strong that 'every independent act of the Dönitz government' was intended to 'embroil the Allies with the Russians', decided to send his political adviser to Flensburg. Robert Murphy would look at the situation and help him to make his decision on Dönitz's future. Churchill, for his part, ordered his planning committee to consider the possibilities of 'taking on Russia, should trouble arise in our future discussions with her' (as Brooke described it).

Meanwhile far away in East Berlin a bearded ex-carpenter who was one day to become the most hated man in Central Europe began to work out on paper the tactics for his little exiled Communist group which had arrived in Berlin from Russia a few days before. Comrade Ulbricht, the man who would one day build the infamous Wall and make a mockery of everything that Eisenhower stood and fought for, wrote boldly and unashamedly in his directive which would be issued on the same day that Eisenhower ordered the arrest of the Dönitz Administration: 'It[8] must look democratic. But we've got to have everything in our power first.'

Unknown to Ulbricht, they already had.


IV


Dönitz's big black Mercedes—it had once been Hitler's and had somehow or other found its way from Berlin to Flensburg—drew up at the quay. On the deck of the SS *Patria,* which housed the Allied team attached to his Headquarters, the guard of honour sprang to attention. As the Admiral descended from his car and made his way to the gangplank, the Chief Petty Officer snapped out an order in English, and Dönitz 'came alongside' to the accompaniment of the shrill sound of the bosun's pipes. On deck an American colonel saluted him smartly and with all the ceremony due to a visiting head of state Grand Admiral Dönitz was ushered downstairs to the big cabin where Robert Murphy—'the diplomat among the warriors', as he considered himself—and General Rooks, the American chief of the Allied team, were waiting for him.

'Bob' Murphy kept this first meeting with Dönitz on 17 May purposefully short. He wanted to size up the German initially and then decide what to do. He confined himself to asking Dönitz for his legitimation as head of the 'new government' and was handed copies of the message Bormann had sent the Admiral. Glancing through them briefly he nodded his head approvingly and let Dönitz speak. With his typical blindness to reality and his inability to understand the political facts of life—namely that he was already regarded by the American allies as a war criminal and potential prisoner—Dönitz launched into a long diatribe about the impending 'bolshevification' of Europe.

Rooks and Murphy listened in silence and Dönitz thought their attitude was 'reserved but correct'. In fact the two Americans were highly alarmed by Dönitz's words; they interpreted them as just another German attempt—this time at the highest level—to create trouble between the Western and Soviet Allies. But Dönitz chattered on, showing a complete lack of insight into the mentality of most Anglo-Americans who

8. The Communist takeover of power.

thought of the Russians as trusted Allies who had borne most of the fighting in World War II. Murphy and Rooks exchanged glances every now and again, but otherwise they did not interrupt.

In the end the three of them agreed to meet on the following day at Dönitz's HQ and the Admiral left, apparently believing that he had 'made a good impression' on the Americans, as he confidently reported to Lüdde-Neurath.

Albert Speer was not blinded by the apparent friendliness of the Allied team. He had already made up his mind to leave the Dönitz 'government'. He regarded his fellow 'cabinet' members with contempt as men 'trying to offset their unimportance by sham activity'. Every morning they met at ten in the 'cabinet room'—a former classroom where they sat on the painted wooden children's chairs around a schoolroom table much too small for them—and more often than not their 'discussions' developed into drinking sessions to which the 'Minister of Food' would bring bottles of rye from his private store. So the day would pass with the cabinet drinking itself into a pleasant sense of false security out of cracked toothglasses and chipped cups.

In the end Albert Speer, perhaps the most brilliant of the technocrats who had served Hitler, gave up. On the same day that Eisenhower discussed the fate of the Dönitz 'Government' with Churchill, he wrote Schwerin von Krosigk a letter of resignation, stating that it 'was as foolish to entrust an artist[9] with paying off the debts of the past as to put a champagne salesman (von Ribbentrop) in charge of the Foreign Ministry.' He finished the letter with the request that he be 'relieved of the affairs of the Minister of Economics and Production'.

But there was no reply to his communication and in the end he simply left Flensburg, slipped through the Allied cordon and joined his family at the Castle of Glücksburg—there to await for the inevitable last act of the farce in Flensburg.

On the day that Rooks, accompanied by his British deputy, General Foord, arrived at Dönitz's HQ in the Mürwik Barracks, all the Nazi flags and Hitler busts had been carefully removed. The guard presented arms and the two Generals were ushered into Dönitz's office. The discussion could begin.

But again it was not a discussion but a speech by Dönitz in which he developed his theories about the necessity of German co-operation with the Western Allies in the face of the Russian

9. Speer always considered him an artist—as did Hitler.

threat. It was an attitude that was no longer new to the two politely listening Allied officers. The first Allied visitor to Dönitz's HQ, young Major Howarth of Montgomery's staff, who had gone there before the war had officially ended, had reported that a German colonel in intelligence had put forward the same line 'over bad sausage and even worse schnapps'. Strong, Eisenhower's Chief-of-Intelligence, had warned them what to expect. But they said nothing and let Dönitz talk.

'I told you yesterday,' he said, 'that in the last months of the war up to the capitulation a flood of refugees fled from the East because of their fear of the Russians. There was an anti-Russian feeling in the whole German people. The people thought, if we could only have peace with the West, we would fight against the Russians with all the means at our disposal. This attitude has changed today among those Germans who live in the areas occupied by yourselves. In all sections of the populace there is an ever-growing point of view which says "Why don't we go in with the Bolsheviks?"

'Already a large part of the labour force think that way. In Hamburg they have already hoisted a large number of red flags. Trucks and motor cycles drive through the city bearing red flags. This tendency to go in with Russia had already reached the middle class and many nationalistic circles. Even in the Army there is a growing feeling that the right way is to go in with Russia...'

With growing scepticism the two Generals listened to Dönitz; they knew better than he did what was going on in Hamburg, but the Admiral obviously believed his own words.

'We are getting more and more reports,' Dönitz rambled on, 'that rebuilding is going ahead faster in the Russian Occupation Zone. The subway is running again in Berlin and the railway in the countryside. The German workers can express themselves freely. They are playing German music again and treating the people well, giving them cigarettes and refreshments.'

He then went on to compare this kind of treatment with that which the Germans were receiving in the West, with its emphasis on Belsen and Dachau and the crimes committed by the Nazis. He added bitterly that, he, personally, was being constantly defamed in the Allied press, something which had never happened during the war. Even at the height of the conflict, his submarine campaign had always been regarded by the Allied press as 'hard but fair'. Now the British and Americans were calling him a 'war criminal' in their newspapers.

Thus it went on for one whole hour until he ended his diatribe with the threat that 'you have the power. What you do with me is your affair. But you must understand that *then* (he meant presumably if he were officially regarded as a war criminal) my influence on the *Wehrmacht* will vanish.' On that note he allowed the Allied generals to depart. After they had gone he told Lüdde-Neurath that they were 'obviously impressed'.

They were. But *not* in the manner he anticipated. Returning to the *SS Patria* they conferred with Robert Murphy and then forwarded their recommendation to Eisenhower. It was simple enough—Dönitz must go.

### v

While Dönitz still lived in hopes of coming to some arrangement with the Allies that would secure his position in Flensburg, others of the Nazi *Prominenz* had already realized that the end was near. Some, like the brutal ex-Reich Commissioner of the Ukraine, Koch, had demanded a submarine from Dönitz in which they could flee the impending Russian revenge. Rosenberg, the oldest *Reichsleiter* in the Party, looked for a way out in drink, being found almost lifeless one evening in Mürwik. The doctors suspected that he had poisoned himself. He had—but with alcohol—and survived to stand trial at Nuremberg, where one year later an imprisoned Speer would declare bitterly of the lot of them: 'Yes, I know—they made great heroic speeches about fighting and dying for the Fatherland without risking their own necks. And now when their own lives are at stake, they shiver and look for all kinds of excuses—so that's the kind of heroes we had leading Germany to destruction!'

One of those heroes, Heinrich Himmler, had already disappeared. A few days before, SS General Ohlendorf had protested to him, 'You can't just walk out! You must make a radio speech or send some declaration to the Allies that you take responsibility for what's happened. You must give the reasons!'

Himmler had avoided any argument and had gone to see Schwerin von Krosigk, 'Please tell me what is going to become of me?' he had asked plaintively.

'I'm not interested in the least what will happen to you or any other man,' von Krosigk had snapped, and had gone on to tell him he should commit suicide or disappear with a false beard. He did exactly that. He shaved off his moustache, put a patch over one eye and, changing his name to Heinrich Hitzinger, set off with several companions to try and escape.

For two weeks they wandered through the chaotic backroads and farm tracks of Schleswig-Holstein, nothing to distinguish them from the other hundreds of thousands of refugees save their vehicles. They crossed the Elbe by bribing a fisherman and were now about 100 miles from Flensburg. On 21 May they were preparing to bluff their way through the checkpoint set up by the British at Bremervörde. But to do so they knew they needed travel documents. They decided, therefore, to send one of their party, Kiermaier, to the British office for these documents. If he were arrested the others would slip away.

Kiermaier was arrested and the rest fled. But they did not make a successful escape. Soon all of them, still jealously guarding their new and faked identities, were inmates in 031 Civilian Interrogation Camp near Lüneburg.

Captain Tom Selvester, who was commandant of the Camp, was suspicious when he heard from an NCO that three of the new arrivals from Bremervörde were kicking up a fuss, demanding to see him at once; usually the Nazi suspects were only too eager to ingratiate themselves with their guards by good behaviour. He ordered the three of them to be brought to his office that afternoon.

The first man to enter was, in Selvester's own words, 'small, ill-looking and shabbily dressed'. The men who followed him were obviously soldiers. The British Captain recognized that stiff-backed, trained look immediately. He ordered them to be taken away and kept in close custody and then turned his attention to the small man wearing the black patch over his left eye. But before he could start his interrogation the little man removed the patch and put on a pair of spectacles. Selvester's heart skipped a beat. He knew *that* face!

'Heinrich Himmler,' the little man introduced himself in a quiet voice.

## VI

On that same afternoon, 22 May, 1945 Lt-Commander Lüdde-Neurath received an unexpected telephone call from the *SS Patria*. The British interpreter was brief and to the point. After introducing himself, he said simply, 'Tell Admiral Dönitz that General Rooks would like to see him tomorrow morning at zero nine forty-five hours—*precisely!*' With that he hung up.

Lüdde-Neurath replaced the telephone and crossed over to the Admiral's office. Dönitz looked up from his papers and Lüdde-Neurath repeated the Allied message. For what seemed a long time, Dönitz was silent, seemingly digesting the news. Slowly a faint smile appeared on his thin lips. 'Neurath,' he said simply, 'pack the bags!'

He knew what the summons meant—the end of Karl Dönitz and his government.

# 3

## Finale at Flensburg

### WEDNESDAY, 23 MAY, 1945

'Comment is superfluous.'

*Admiral Dönitz*

I

On the morning of 23 May a French fishing boat approached the tiny island of Minquiers, one of the Channel Island group. It was the first time that the French fishermen had sailed these waters for over five years and they were looking forward to a record catch. Lucien Marie, captain of *Les Trois Fréres*, on watch on the bridge, suddenly became aware that the island—a collection of low reefs—was inhabited. He was surprised. He had thought there was no one on the island since the Germans had gone. He announced to his small crew, 'It looks as if the English have taken possession.'

One of them cursed. Before the war the French and English fishermen had fought over the island and its very desirable fishing ground often enough; in fact they had been doing so for nearly a century.

'Don't say they're out fishing,' someone exclaimed.

'No,' the skipper answered. 'They look like Tommies ... I think they're wearing uniforms. Let's have a look at them.'

A few minutes later the little boat weighed anchor off the nearest reef and the crew of *Les Trois Fréres* waded ashore to where a small group of soldiers waited curiously. Abruptly Captain Marie stopped. The men were Germans, and they were armed!

Bewildered by the sight of an armed enemy nearly three weeks after the surrender, the Frenchman wondered what he should do. He didn't have to wait long. The nearest German, a sergeant, raised his pistol and said in fairly good Norman French, 'Hey you, come here!'

While the rest of the crew slowly raised their hands, the

Skipper walked over hesitantly. 'What is it?' he asked.

'Listen, Frenchman,' the German said. 'We've been forgotten by the British. Perhaps no one in Jersey told them we were here.'

Marie nodded but said nothing.

'So, now we've had enough. We are running out of food and water. You must help us.'

'How?' Marie asked.

'Simple. I want you to take us over to England.' He hesitated. 'We want to surrender.'

Thus the last armed German at large west of the River Elbe passed into Allied captivity to join the rest of *Division Kanada* in the place they forecast they would end up—Canada.[1]

II

At precisely quarter to ten on that same morning the Grand Admiral's car drove up to the *SS Patria*. Lüdde-Neurath opened the door and his chief got out. This time there was no Allied colonel to welcome them on the gangplank and no guard to present arms. Now the British infantrymen eyed them coldly and motionlessly as they crossed the cobbles of the quayside. Imperceptibly Dönitz shrugged at the discourtesy. He began to mount the gangplank while above them on the deck the uniformed correspondents with their notebooks and the photographers with their cameras jostled each other for a better position. Dönitz looked significantly at his adjutant. He had been right.

The interpreter ushered them into the ship's bar which had been rearranged as a conference room, where they waited for five minutes until the Allied generals came in—Rooks followed by Foord and the Russian General Truskov. Today the Russian was no longer smiling as he had been when he first made his appearance at Dönitz's HQ and hoped he would win the Germans over. His face today was set and grim. Evidently he had received a new set of orders from Moscow.

1. There is talk that there were pockets of armed resistance later than this date. But apart from Soviet complaints that German mountain troops were still active and armed in Norway in late September and the certainty that all the Werewolves did not surrender till about the same date, the author could not find any confirmation.

The three Generals took their seats with Rooks in the centre. Dönitz seated himself opposite.

Lowell Rooks rose and began to read from the paper in his hand. His voice was slightly raised and awkward, as if he were not accustomed to reading aloud. 'Gentlemen,' he announced, 'I am in receipt of instructions from Supreme Headquarters, European Theater of Operations, from the Supreme Commander General Eisenhower, to call you before me this morning to tell you that he has decided, in concert with the Soviet High Command, that today the acting German Government and the German High Command, with the several of its members shall be taken into custody as prisoners of war. Thereby the acting German Government is dissolved.'

He stopped and looked over the top of the paper at the Admiral. But there was no reaction. Dönitz's English was not good enough for him to understand the full meaning. Rooks continued:

'When you leave this room an Allied officer will attach himself to you and escort you to your quarters where you will pack, have your lunch and complete your affairs, after which they will escort you to the airfield at one-thirty for emplaning. You may take the baggage you require. That's all I have to say.'

The American put his paper down and let the interpreter take over. When the latter was finished, he looked directly at Dönitz and asked: 'Would you like to make a statement?'

The Admiral shook his head: 'Comment is superfluous,' he said simply.

It was all over in a matter of minutes. Followed by von Friedeburg and his Adjutant he clattered down the gangplank to the accompaniment of whirring cameras and the pop of flashbulbs. No Allied escorting officer was waiting for him below. Accordingly he turned to von Friedeburg whose eyes were full of tears and put his hand on the other man's shoulder. 'I don't think I can stand the circus which is about to begin,' the smaller Admiral said.

Depressed himself, Dönitz tried to cheer his old comrade up. 'We will be treated as prisoners of war under the terms of the Geneva Convention,' he urged. 'You must not take everything so tragically.'

Apparently consoled by Dönitz's words the chief negotiator wandered off to his own car. Still there was no sign of the escorting officer. In the end Dönitz—always a stickler for punctuality—ordered his driver to leave. Moments later

Lüdde-Neurath looked out of the rear window of the Mercedes to see a young officer in American Navy uniform come running frantically out of a nearby building. When he saw that his charge had gone, he dashed to the nearest military vehicle and commandeered it, ordering the driver to follow Dönitz. It was all very much like the old American gangster movies the Admiral remembered seeing before the war. Amused in spite of his depressed mood, he tapped his driver on the shoulder and said: 'Slow down a little. We don't want to get the poor chap into trouble.'


### III

Almost at that moment Schwerin von Krosigk had opened his daily 'cabinet' meeting and was launched upon the most pressing political problems of the day when the door of the room in the ex-school-house was flung open. British soldiers rushed in. They were heavily armed with grenades and stens. 'Out—and put your hands up!' they ordered. Surprised and in some cases startled out of their wits, the assembled civilians and soldiers did as they were told. Quickly the soldiers of the 11th Armoured lined them up along the wall of the corridor outside. They were frisked expertly and then came the command which shocked the German dignitaries: 'Hosen' runter!' Schwerin von Krosigk's mouth fell open. 'Pants down!'—what did they mean?

He soon found out. A tough little soldier smelling of carbolic soap and cheap tobacco tugged at his trousers. 'Bitte ... please!' the German aristocrat and former Rhodes Scholar stuttered. But it was no use. Everywhere the soldiers were forcing the Germans to drop their trousers to their ankles, so that a sergeant, his finger encased in a rubber surgical stool, could search their anus for a concealed capsule of poison.

Under the command of Brigadier Churcher three battalions of infantry had now taken up positions around the Flensburg Enclave arresting anybody and everybody connected with the Dönitz Regime. Hundreds of them were forced, hands above their heads, into the square of the Mürwik Barracks, where they were subjected to the cross-questioning of the assembled correspondents and the snap and flash of the photographers.

Speer, who had been arrested by a British sergeant at Glücksburg—the NCO had taken his pistol off and laid it on the table while Speer packed—was now also present. He thought

171

the new prisoners, including himself, 'must have looked like emigrants waiting for their ship'.

Then it was his turn to submit to the physical examination. He was 'affronted by the embarrassing' body search, but thought later it was 'probably a consequence of Himmler's suicide'.

But as yet Heinrich Himmler was not dead. He was in the interrogation centre under the charge of Sergeant-Major Austin, dressed in his underpants and shirt and covered by a grey army blanket.

'That's your bed,' the NCO said. 'Get undressed.'

Himmler did not seem to understand although Austin spoke German.

'He doesn't know who I am,' he said to the interpreter.

'Yes I do,' Austin broke in. 'You're Himmler. All the same that's your bed. Get undressed!'

A little later Colonel Murphy of Intelligence and the MO, Doctor Wells, came in to carry out yet another search to ensure that Himmler had no poison hidden on his person. Finally the two of them had a look at his mouth again. Suddenly Murphy saw 'a small black knob sticking out between the gap in the teeth on the right-hand side lower jaw'.

'Come nearer the light,' the doctor ordered. 'Open your mouth.'

He thrust two fingers in Himmler's mouth. The latter suddenly pressed down and bit hard. 'Ouch!' Wells yelled. *'He's done it!'*

Murphy and Austin jumped on Himmler. They flung him on the ground, rolling him on his stomach to prevent him swallowing the poison. Wells strangled him trying to make him spit it out while Murphy shouted for a needle and cotton. It came with remarkable speed. In great haste the Colonel threaded the needle. Without hesitation he stuck the metal through Himmler's tongue and tugged it out of his dying mouth. Meanwhile Wells was using his stomach pump and at the same time administering emetics. But the Chief of the SS was failing fast. Desperately the doctor tried artificial respiration. But then, as Sergeant-Major Austin recorded for the BBC the following day, 'He died and when he died we threw a blanket over him and left him.'[2]

2. Two days later he was buried in a spot known only to Sgt-Major Austin, wrapped in army blankets and wound in camouflage netting secured with telephone wire. Today the NCO is the only man who knows where the ex-chicken farmer who had ravaged half of Europe is buried.

Heinrich Himmler was not the only suicide that day. Pudgy Admiral von Friedeburg had just taken the salute of a party of German marines who had marched past singing the proud defiant song of the good years, *Wir Fahren Gegen England,* when his eye fell on the scene below in the square where his ex-comrades huddled, hands above their heads. He asked his escort if he could go to the lavatory. The Allied officer approved, and five minutes later the man who had negotiated the surrender was dead, poisoned by cyanide.

Immediately his body (according to German sources) was plundered by the soldiers, and the panic-stricken American escorting officer, appalled by the fact he had lost his charge, seized von Friedeburg's young aide and imprisoned him as a substitute for the dead Commander-in-Chief of the German Navy.[3]

An ashen-faced Admiral Dönitz heard the news in silence. On this black day everything—and anything—was possible. Already he had been shoved out of his house, had his bejewelled Grand Admiral's baton stolen and his baggage rifled. Now he too was to be subjected to the final indignity. He and Jodl, the two men who had done so much to bring the mighty British Empire almost to its knees in the middle years of the war, were also to be forced to undergo the anal search.

## IV

In London Winston Churchill, who was soon to write in protest to Montgomery that 'I did not like to see German admirals and generals with whom we had recently made arrangements being made to stand with their hands above their heads. Nor did I like to see the infantry component of the 11th Armoured Division used in this particular task,'[4] also had an unpleasant duty to perform that afternoon. He was to hand in his resignation to the King at Buckingham Palace, whose Empire, the greatest the world had ever seen and ever would, he

3. This unfortunate officer was to go through all the stages of treatment reserved for high Nazi war criminals until he was finally released at Nuremberg.

4. He added 'I understand the whole was ordered from SHAEF'. Presumably Churchill thought that the affair was intended to humiliate the Germans in the eyes of the Russians and clarify any doubts that the latter might have about American intentions towards Dönitz.

was trying so desperately to save, not only from enemies but also from 'friends'. Of course he knew that the King would empower him to form a transitional 'caretaker' government, but would it survive the coming general election?

In his office in the 'War House' Sir Alan Brooke, Chief of the Imperial General Staff, worried too about the future that afternoon. With him he had the planners' report on 'the possibility of taking on Russia'. Churchill had ordered it drawn up in case 'trouble should arise in our future discussions with her (Russia)'.

But even before he had really had time to read it thoroughly, he knew that 'the idea is, of course, fantastic and the chances of success quite impossible'. Wearily he concluded that, 'There is no doubt that from now onwards Russia is all-powerful in Europe'.

And not far away Montgomery, the newly appointed head of the British Zone of Occupation who knew that the 'British people were completely fed up with the war' and could never be persuaded 'to fight the Russians', briefed the civilian heads of his new German administration who would soon be crossing over to Germany. While in the American Zone of Occupation the official policy was to be one of retribution to make the Germans pay for their crimes, he told his officials that day that 'we must get civil control re-established' and that that 'would mean the civil divisions of the Control Commmission dealing with the Germans themselves'.

Soon he would return himself to Germany and begin to run his part of it like he had run his own 21st Army Group—like a military formation so that back in Whitehall, the authorities started to think he was turning into 'a military dictator who would seize power' (as he wrote himself later). To the very end Field-Marshal Montgomery was suspect, the wrong man doing the right things.

v

In Flensburg it was almost over now. That same evening the leaders, Dönitz, Jodl, Speer and the rest of the *Prominenz* were driven to Flensburg airport under a forty-vehicle escort. There they were ordered into an American DC-4 to be flown off to their place of imprisonment.

For the last time the photographers clustered around them to take shots before they departed; and there is a final photograph of Admiral Dönitz on that day of disgrace, crouched amid the metallic jungle of the plane's interior, sitting between the suitcases and packing cases. His face bears a slight smile—a mixture of despair and cynicism—and tells better than any of his later words that he had realized that the dream was over. Before him lay the bitter agony of the trial at Nuremberg and the long, long years of prison. A little later they took off and flew over the North Sea. Behind them they left a Germany in ruins, its conquered people cowed and disorganized among the rubble of their once proud country, now at the mercy of the two new great super-powers who would do with it what they wished.

Slowly as the plane cruised southwards—possibly towards London, Speer thought—Dönitz, Jodl and the rest began to realize that they were no longer the actors who had played such a great role in their nation's supreme drama. The grand illusion had collapsed. The colossal performance of the 'Thousand Year Empire', which had lasted exactly twelve years, was over. In the bitter years ahead they and their people would look back at this time and wonder if it ever could conceivably have taken place: that gigantic dream with its loud-mouthed effrontery, gold-braided vulgarity, jack-booted cruelty—the bloody nobility of its youthful sacrifices. It was all over.

It was dark when they arrived at Luxemburg Airport. A cordon of American soldiers was drawn up waiting for them. Each man had an automatic rifle aimed at the lane through which they would walk to the open 'deuce and a half' trucks. Speer thought he had seen 'such a reception only in gangster films when the criminals are finally led off to justice'.

They drove swiftly through Luxemburg City, headlights ablaze at last, the mobs hooting them. On through the steep hills, filled with the heady scent of pine. On and on towards Germany. But the long line of trucks did not cross the border which was the River Moselle. They stopped instead at the little riverside resort of Bad Mondorf at the heavily guarded Palast Hotel, set back in its own park.

From outside Speer could see the other *Prominenten* of the Third Reich—Goering and the rest—pacing up and down the barred, but glass-windowed verandah. They were all there— the ministers, the field marshals, the state secretaries. For Speer, staring at them from outside, 'It was a ghostly experience to find all those who at the end had scattered like chaff in the wind reassembled here.' But he had no time to reflect further. The guards pushed him forward into what the German prisoners with their keen sense of their own social standing named the *Prominentenlager*.

The GIs who guarded them allowed their prisoners no such pretensions. With brutal directness they gave the hotel camp their own title. It was *Camp Ashcan*!

It was nearly midnight when Admiral Dönitz was finally able to settle down alone in his room, undisturbed now save for the measured soft tread of the sentries outside in the park. Tossing and turning in the unaccustomed bed, a myriad thoughts flooding his troubled mind, the old sailor finally fell asleep. Silence settled on the prison.

Three thousand miles away in New York an American newspaperman Drew Middleton scribbled away furiously at his article for the morning's *New York Times*. It would begin quite simply with the sentence: 'THE THIRD REICH DIED TODAY.'

# Selected Bibliography

Bradley, O., *A Soldier's Story*, Holt.
Bryant, A., *The Turn of the Tide*, Vols I and II, Collins.
Butcher, H., *My Three Years with Eisenhower*, Simon & Schuster.
*By Air to Battle*, H.M.S.O.
Churchill, W., *The Second World War*, Houghton Mifflin.
Clarke, D., *The Eleventh at War*, Collins.
Codman, C., *Drive*, Little Brown,
de Guingand, F., *Operation Victory*, Hodder & Stoughton.
Der Vils, *Tragedie Op Texel*, Langeveld.
Eisenhower, D., *Crusade in Europe*, Doubleday.
———,' *The Papers of Dwight Eisenhower*, Johns Hopkins Press.
Essame, H., *The Battle for Germany*, Scribners.
———, *History of the 43rd Wessex Division*.
Farago, L., *Patton*, Obolensky.
Hansen, R., *Das Ende des Britten Reiches*, Universitat Kiel (Klett).
*History of the 7th Armored*.
Horrocks, B., *A Full Life*, Collins.
Ingersoll, R., *Top Secret*, Harcourt Brace.
Manvell, R. & Fraenkel, H., *Himmler*, Mentor.
Maugham, R., *Jersey Under the Jackboot*, Corgi.
Montgomery, B., *Memoirs*, Collins.
Moorehead, A., *Montgomery*, Collins.
Mordal, J., *Hold-Up Naval à Granville*, Edition France Empire.
Murphy, R., *Diplomat Among the Warriors*, Collins.

Neurath, L., *Regierung Donitz,* Musterschmidt.
Patton, G., *War as I Knew It,* Houghton Mifflin.
Ryan, C., *The Last Battle,* Four Square.
Saunders, H., *Red Beret,* Michael Joseph.
————, *Green Beret,* Michael Joseph.
Scarfe, N., *Assault Division,* Collins.
Speer, *Memoirs,* Weidenfeld & Nicolson.
Steinert, M., *Die 23 Tage der Regierung Donitz,* Econ.
*The Story of the 9th Army,* Infantry Press.
Strong, K., *Intelligence at the Top,* Cassell.
Summersby, K., *Eisenhower Was My Boss,* Dell.
*Taurus Pursuant: History of the 11th Armored Division.*
Thompson, R., *Montgomery Legend,* Allen & Unwin.
Thorwald, J., *Das Ende an der Elbe,* Steingruben.
Toland, J., *The Last 100 Days,* Random House.
*The 12th Yorkshire Parachute Battalion in Germany.*
*War History of the 4th Bn King's Own Scottish Borders.*
Whiting, C., *Bradley,* Ballantine.
————, *Hitler's Werewolves,* Stein and Day.
Wilmot, C., *The Struggle for Europe,* Greenwood.